BEST DAY ON EARTH

CONTENTS

SUNRISE 8-51

Whether you're watching fishermen on the placid waters of Inle Lake, taking a hot-air balloon ride over medieval Rocamadour or drifting along the River Ganges, getting up early will reward you with beautiful light and mercifully uncrowded spaces.

DAYTIME 52-167

There are countless ways to fill your day: get face-to-face with mountain gorillas in the forests of Rwanda, climb strange clusters of boulders in Joshua Tree National Park, or go wild with the locals at Buñol's tomato-throwing festival.

SUNSET 168–209

Everything looks better at sunset, but everyone has a special one they remember: it could be eagles taking flight off Atlantic cliffs in Portugal, lions prowling at dusk in the Serengeti, or the tropical sky bursting into colour in the Maldives.

AFTER DARK 210–253

As night falls you'll find city skylines sparkling from Hong Kong to Chicago, street food tantalizing your tastebuds from Marrakesh to Laos, and partygoers filling the streets of Rio or lining up for the ultimate club night in Ibiza.

INTRODUCTION

As you read this, someone, somewhere will be watching the sun set over the horizon. Others will be up after dark, dancing or counting the stars in perfect silence, while early risers will gaze eastward, waiting for a new day of adventures to begin. At any given moment there are a thousand and one extraordinary travel experiences to be had. You just need to know where to look.

So where to begin your Best Day on Earth? With a group of climbers taking their final steps to the summit of Mount Kilimanjaro, their breath condensing in the freezing dawn light? Or in a hot-air balloon, drifting over the unearthly fairy chimneys of Cappadocia in Turkey? And what better way to end the day than by watching pools of bronze light and shadow play across the Grand Canyon at dusk, or by strolling along the Mekong River in Laos as the smell of street food fills the air?

Right now, somewhere, there's also a Rough Guides author hitting the road to research one of our guidebooks or write a feature for our award-winning website. We have dozens of travel experts dotted across the globe – from Brooklyn to Borneo – and this book is a snapshot of some of their favourite experiences. Of course, we've only scratched the surface of all the wonderful things you can see and do in 24 hours, but we hope that what we have chosen inspires you to book a ticket, travel somewhere new and have your very own Best Day on Earth.

LOCATION MAP

Planning the Best Day on Earth involves a fair bit of mental globe-trotting so we've produced a handy map to plot your adventure. If you're wondering where Tajikistan or Gabon is look no further – each experience is colour-coded and listed with a page and photo number so you can quickly find what you're after.

Map markers: 109, 009, 102, 140, 050, 114, 023, 142, 156, 121, 028, 006, 053, 110, 070, 067, 079, 052, 047, 096, 065, 084, 141, 057, 085, 020, 027, 017, 101, 056, 106, 151, 069, 048

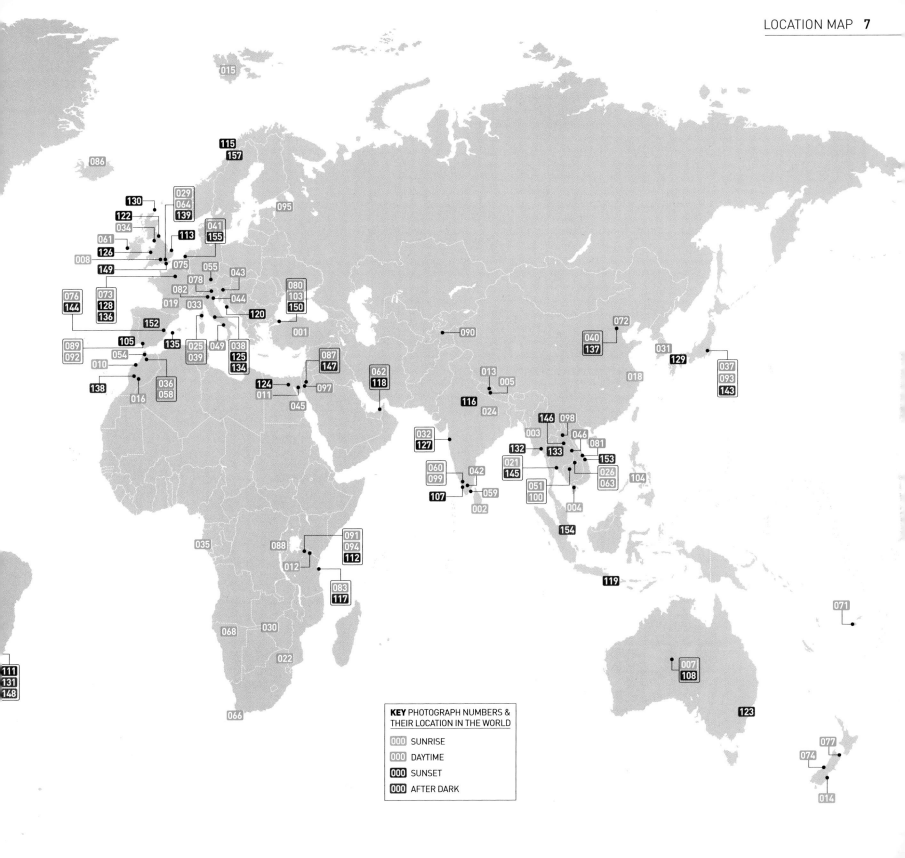

KEY PHOTOGRAPH NUMBERS &
THEIR LOCATION IN THE WORLD

000 SUNRISE
000 DAYTIME
000 SUNSET
000 AFTER DARK

SUNRISE

Whether you're watching fishermen on the placid waters of Inle Lake, taking a hot-air balloon ride over medieval Rocamadour or drifing along the River Ganges, getting up early will reward you with beautiful light and mercifully uncrowded spaces.

001

MARVEL AT OTHERWORLDLY CAPPADOCIA

TURKEY Cappadocia's surreal landscape is no secret. It baffles with a whole host of peculiar rock formations, from ancient underground cities and ochre-red canyons peppered with rock-cut churches, to the famous "fairy chimneys" – soft, dusty rock spires that jut 30m skyward. And it feels even more unearthly at first light. Few people can resist the temptation to soak up a panorama while flying over the land in a hot-air balloon; however, the views are also stunning from the ground. Roused by a spine-tingling dawn call to prayer, you can watch as a kaleidoscope of brightly coloured hot-air balloons fills the sky and sweeps over the lunar landscape of plunging valleys, high plateaus and burrowed dwellings.

002

WATCH STILT FISHERMEN AT WORK

SRI LANKA The sun-baked south coast of Sri Lanka remains essentially rural: a land of a thousand sleepy villages sheltered under innumerable palms, where the laidback pace of life still revolves around coconut farming, rice cultivation and the distinctively Sri Lankan art of stilt fishing. Near the island's southernmost tip the town of Ahangama is famous for having the greatest concentration of stilt fishermen. The stilts consist of a single pole and crossbar planted out in the sea, on which fishermen perch while casting their lines when the currents are flowing in the right direction. Positions are highly lucrative thanks to the abundant supplies of fish, even close to shore, and are handed down from father to son. Get up early to see them at work, elegantly silhouetted against a plum-coloured sky.

003

SEE DAWN BREAK OVER BAGAN

MYANMAR Studded with more than two thousand Buddhist structures across a 67-square-kilometre stretch of dusty plain, the sheer size of Myanmar's ancient capital is overwhelming. In fact, it's so packed full of temples, pagodas and monasteries that in some places it is impossible to walk between the buildings. A must-visit sight at any time of day, arguably Bagan is most enchanting at dawn when its magical vistas truly come into their own. Whether you stay on the ground or take to the sky in a hot-air balloon, the views enchant. Watch as the sun's rays seep through the hazy sky, and ornate spires and pagodas, partially cloaked in the low-lying mist, are slowly unveiled.

004

HAGGLE AT CAI RANG FLOATING MARKET

VIETNAM Base yourself at Can Tho – the Mekong Delta's biggest city – a great jumping-off point for the area's best floating markets and the ideal place to spend the night before an early start out on the water. Wake up in the dark and get a boat 6km along the river to Cai Rang. By 5am the delta's biggest floating market is already a hive of activity. Approaching the market, the dawn illuminates a swarming armada of brightly painted boats, all laden with fresh, seasonal produce, weaving between each other in an intricate series of waterways. Despite the bustle, navigation is relatively easy, as each boat advertises its wares atop a bamboo mast.

005

RENT A DOONGA ON PHEWA TAL

NEPAL The Himalayas make the greatest rise from subtropical valley floor to icy summit of any mountain range on Earth, and the contrast is stunningly apparent at Phewa Tal (Phewa Lake). Rent a brightly painted *doonga* (boat) first thing in the morning to watch the first rays of light hit the 8000m-plus Annapurna and Manaslu ranges, looming almost touchably 25km to the north. According to a local legend, Phewa Tal covers the area of a once-prosperous valley, whose inhabitants one day scorned a wandering beggar. Finding only one sympathetic woman, the beggar warned her of an impending flood. As the woman and her family fled to higher ground, a torrent roared down from the mountains and submerged the town – the "beggar" having been none other than the goddess Barahi Bhagwati.

006

WAKE UP IN THE MOJAVE DESERT

USA There's nothing quite like waking up to dawn breaking over the barren panorama of the Mojave Desert. Desolate, silent and virtually lifeless, this is the mythic badland of the West. Apart from the huge dust-covered trucks that trundle across the state to Nevada and beyond, your only company here is likely to be hardcore bikers and neo-hippies. The immense Mojave National Preserve makes an ideal spot to take a break from the freeway and camp out for a night or two. Once the sun has risen, explore your surroundings. Scrambling around the spectacular Kelso Dunes, a golden 8km stretch reaching as high as 200m, is fun but disorientating: with nothing man-made to compare them to, these vast mountains of sand can certainly skew your sense of perspective.

007

WATCH THE UNVEILING OF ULURU

AUSTRALIA From fridge magnets and key rings, to postcards and T-shirts, almost everywhere you go in Australia you will find the image of Uluru plastered across tourist paraphernalia. So it's no surprise that this popular rock can seem all too familiar, and even underwhelming, when you finally get to see it. But the experience of watching dawn break over Australia's icon will sear an image in your memory no souvenir can tarnish. Surrounded by a barren landscape, watch as the charcoal sky blends through purples, greens, pinks and blues, and the great hulking monolith emerges from the darkness. Now visible, colours flit across Uluru's vast sandstone surface, before the harsh full-lit daylight delivers it to a recognizable baked-orange hue.

008

CATCH SUNRISE AT STONEHENGE

ENGLAND One of England's most famous, and most controversial, ancient sites, people flock year-round to visit this strange ring of megaliths. Without the crowds, at dawn the mystery of the place can be felt most keenly. Most unmissable, however, is the chance to experience Stonehenge at the summer solstice. Structurally aligned towards the point of sunrise at this time, this annual spectacle draws an eclectic group of 35,000 or more visitors to Stonehenge. No longer held back by the official ropes that cordon off the stones at other times, white-robed worshipping Druids, pagans on pilgrimage, perplexed families and partying teens crowd within the inner stone circle to witness the sunrise on the longest day of the year.

009

START THE DAY IN KATMAI NATIONAL PARK

USA Summer is the ideal time to explore Alaska's awe-inspiring wilderness of deep fjords, towering glaciers and sweeping forests. And Katmai National Park is an obvious draw: a remote and bewilderingly beautiful stretch of volcanic landscape, punctuated with some still-smoking cones and crammed with wildlife. Experiencing the sunrise here – especially one reflected in a crystal-clear lake – is breathtakingly peaceful and makes the perfect start to a day's exploring. Once the sun is up there's a whole host of things to do, from hiking and fishing to kayaking and canoeing. If you are here in July don't miss the sockeye salmon run that lures both brown bears (the park is home to over 2000 of them) and camera-clad visitors to the park.

010

FEEL SMALL AT HASSAN II MOSQUE

MOROCCO If you start your day at Casablanca's Hassan II Mosque it is hard not to be inspired. Raised on a rocky platform reclaimed from the ocean, the mosque is vast. Its minaret is 200m high, making it the tallest in the world – a laser on its summit projects a beam towards Mecca – while the mosque itself provides space for 25,000 worshippers inside, and a further 80,000 in its courtyard. As a building, it's second only to Mecca's in size, and St Peter's in Rome could fit comfortably inside. At dawn it is even more impressive, with the sun's rays seeping between stone archways into the courtyard and the facade glowing golden in the early light.

011

SEE THE LIGHT ON MOUNT SINAI

EGYPT Venerated by Christians, Jews and Muslims as the place where Moses received the Ten Commandments, Mount Sinai overlooks the valley where God is believed to have been heard speaking from a burning bush. While some archeologists question whether this really was the mountain where the Ten Commandments were revealed, the fact that seeing daybreak here will make an impression on you is beyond doubt. Every night pilgrims, travellers and Bedouin guides gather to camp out atop Mount Sinai in preparation for one of the most inspiring sunrises imaginable. Wrap up and hunker down to watch as the rose-tinted light steals across the desert, picking out each craggy granite formation and turning the rocky terrain fiery-red.

012

SCALE THE ROOF OF AFRICA

TANZANIA Numbing cold, high-altitude thin-air and an unsettling midnight departure – there's no question that the treacherous slog up Mount Kilimanjaro requires grim determination. But it's certainly worth it to experience dawn from the summit (Uhuru Peak), which at 5892m holds multiple titles as Africa's highest mountain, the world's tallest free-standing massif and one of the largest volcanoes on Earth. And even better than the raw statistics is the view that greets you on arrival. Once you reach the top, the frosted darkness lifts and the clouds draw back as the hazy sun rises, revealing the panoramic sweep of a seemingly limitless stretch of the Great Rift Valley as dawn breaks over Africa.

013

CAPTURE THE SUN AT ANNAPURNA BASE CAMP

NEPAL The dramatic Annapurna region, north of the tourist hub of Pokhara, has long been one of Nepal's most popular trekking destinations. Covering a 40km stretch of the Himalaya, the mighty Annapurna Himal harbours nine jutting peaks over 7000m, and is crisscrossed with challenging treks. Early in the morning at Annapurna Base Camp (a mere 4130m up), as the sun inches over the black ridge above, bleary-eyed trekkers get their cameras out to capture the gradual illumination of Annapurna I, towering some 4000m above. Due to the construction of new roads in the area, guides have been forced to stake out different routes and explore new areas, such as Dolpo, home to the elusive snow leopard.

014

VISIT THE MYTHICAL BOULDERS OF OTAGO

NEW ZEALAND The Maori believed the large, grey and almost perfectly spherical Moeraki Boulders, on New Zealand's Otago coast, to be food baskets washed ashore from the shipwrecked canoe – in fact a boat-shaped seaward reef – you can see just offshore. These smooth domes of rock – some of them two metres in diameter – hunker on the sandy beach, partially submerged, and reveal honeycomb centres when broken. They were not in fact washed up by the sea, nor did they fall from the sky, but in fact lay deep inside the mudstone cliffs behind the beach. As the sea eroded the cliffs, out fell the boulders; their distinctive fractured surface was formed as further erosion exposed a network of veins.

015

GAZE AT SVALBARD'S MIDNIGHT SUN

NORWAY In few places does the rising sun hold such mystic allure as it does in Svalbard, an otherworldly, barren archipelago located some 836km north of the Norwegian mainland and 1308km south of the North Pole. Between May and August the sun never sets, flooding the archipelago in a continuous stream of light ahead of the long, dark winter months when the sun never rises at all. On crisp summer nights the midnight sun is blinding, yet on foggy nights it forms a red glowing orb that is eerily beautiful. By the beginning of July much of the snow has melted in Svalbard, exposing a barely recognizable landscape of deep valleys covered in wild flowers.

016

CATCH THE MORNING LIGHT AT AÏT BENHADDOU

MOROCCO With its souvenir shops and constant stream of tour groups, Aït Benhaddou is not really the place to catch a glimpse of fading *ksar* life, but it is one of the most spectacular sights of the Atlas, piled upon a low hillock above a shallow, reed-strewn river. Its buildings are among the most elaborately decorated and best preserved in the south; they are less fortified than is usually the case along the Drâa or the Dadès, but, towered and crenellated, and with high, sheer walls of dark red pisé, they must have been near impregnable in this remote hillside site. Get up early in the morning to catch the sunrise, when the town is cloaked in a thousand shades of crimson.

017

ADMIRE HUMAN INGENUITY AT LAKE TITICACA

PERU An undeniably calming and majestic sight, Lake Titicaca is the world's largest high-altitude body of water. An immense region both in terms of its history and the breadth of its magical landscape, the Titicaca Basin makes most people feel like they are on top of the world. At sunrise the views are breathtaking; placid and mirror-like, the water reflects the vast sky back on itself, while all along the horizon – which appears to bend away from you – the green Andean mountains can be seen raising their ancient backs towards the sun. As the daylight spreads, islands are revealed: natural mounds rising from the waters and in places man-made floating islands – substantial platforms of totora reeds that have been inhabited since their construction centuries ago by Uros Indians.

018

FEEL ZEN-LIKE ON THE BUND

CHINA Set on the bank of the Huangpu River, with its grand sweep of colonial edifices, imposing banks and flashy hotels, the Bund was once the feverish commercial heart of old Shanghai. It was also a bustling working harbour, its waters clogged with sailing junks and tea-, silk- and machinery-laden freighters, and its shoreline packed with hawkers, beggars and rich foreigners. Still frenetic today, the Bund is a blur of street vendors, businessmen, and tourists dipping in and out of its luxury stores and high-end hotels. At dawn, however, the strip is more serene. Join in or watch as public t'ai chi sessions welcome the day with slowly circling arms, gently arching postures and controlled contortions.

019

SOAR OVER ROCAMADOUR

FRANCE Take an early-morning hot-air balloon ride in the Lot and you will be treated to panoramic views of one of France's most stunning regions: an area whose charm undoubtedly lies in its picturesque landscapes and dozens of harmonious small towns and villages. From the air you can soar silently over sprawling meadows, oak forest valleys, majestic chateaux and honey-stone villages, and float by the spectacular cliff-top village of Rocamadour. Halfway up a cliff in the deep and abrupt canyon of the Alzou stream, the setting of Rocamadour is hard to beat. Since medieval times the place has been inundated by pilgrims drawn by the tomb of Zacchaeus of Jericho, a Christian hermit, and the supposed miraculous abilities of Rocamadour's Black Madonna. Nowadays, pilgrims are outnumbered by more secular-minded visitors, who fill the lanes lined with shops peddling incongruous souvenirs, but who come here mainly to wonder at the sheer audacity of the town's location, built almost vertically into its rocky backdrop – something best admired from the air. As you sweep past in a hot-air balloon, survey the stone houses, churches and medieval fortress, chiselled into the limestone cliffs, and spare a thought for the poor pilgrims, many of whom climb the 223 steps of the Via Sancta on their knees all the way up to the little Chapelle Notre-Dame where the miracle-working twelfth-century Black Madonna resides.

020

HIKE UP TO MACHU PICCHU

PERU Leaving the comfort of your sleeping bag for an hour or so's hike up a mountain in the darkness may sound far from tempting, but grab your headtorch and persevere. Despite the breathless, groggy, sticky ascent, arriving at Machu Picchu before the hordes of coach tourists descend is a truly unforgettable experience. Once at the top, find a spot to hunker down and watch as the sun rises over the ancient Inca site. As the sun's rays spread across Machu Picchu, stone-carved palaces, temples and steep pathways between terraces are revealed. Framing this is a backdrop of dark-green forested mountains, deeply etched valleys twisted through by the gentle curves of Río Urubamba and in the distance the snowy peaks of Salcantay.

021

BUY THE MORNING'S BLOOMS AT PAK KHLONG TALAT

THAILAND Although it's open 24/7, Bangkok's biggest wholesale flower and vegetable market, Pak Khlong Talat, is at its best before dawn. Prices are lowest at this time, but even if you're not looking to buy anything, early morning is still the most interesting time to visit. Before the day begins, the market gardeners from Thonburi and beyond boat and drive their freshly picked produce across the Chao Phraya ready for sale to shopkeepers, restaurateurs and hoteliers. In the covered halls – which have been used since the nineteenth century – vegetables are piled high, and the flower stalls, selling twenty different varieties of cut orchids and countless other tropical blooms, spill onto the streets along the riverfront.

022

SPOT ANIMALS IN KRUGER NATIONAL PARK

SOUTH AFRICA Undulating grasslands, striking granite hills, dense forests and rock-hewn mountains – Kruger is South Africa's most famous reserve and one of the world's greatest national parks. Packed full of animals, a safari here at times feels like a checklist: lions, elephants, rhinos, leopards, cheetahs, buffalos, giraffes, hippos and zebras all call this place home. And as any enthusiastic wildlife-watcher will know, the Kruger is at its best at sunrise. At this time nocturnal animals are still busying about and the big cats go in for the dramatic kill. And it's stunning; elegant silhouettes of giraffes and impalas pass beneath the sun's huge, hazy orb, their figures set against the blazing, endless sky.

023

VISIT THE LINCOLN MEMORIAL BEFORE THE CROWDS ARRIVE

USA Anchoring the west end of the Mall, the Lincoln Memorial is one of Washington DC's most imposing sites. It's a fitting tribute to the sixteenth US president, who preserved the Union through the Civil War and provided the first step towards ending slavery in the country with his Emancipation Proclamation in 1863. Inside the monument, an enormous, craggy likeness of Lincoln sits firmly grasping the arms of his throne-like chair, deep in thought. Inscriptions of his two most celebrated speeches – the Gettysburg Address and the Second Inaugural Address – are carved on the north and south walls. Visit first thing in the morning to enjoy the memorial at your own pace before the sightseeing crowds start rolling in.

024

TAKE A BOAT ALONG THE GANGES

INDIA Glide through the sacred waters as the great Hindu city of Varanasi eases itself into the new day. Known to the devout as Kashi, "the City of Light", this is India's holiest city and one of the oldest living cities in the world, which throughout its history has attracted pilgrims, sannyasins and religious figures such as the Buddha, Mahavira and the Hindu reformer Shankara. At sunrise, bathed in an orange glow, the flights of stone ghats that line the shores of the River Ganges are awash with gentle colour as crowds of brightly dressed pilgrims and residents perform puja, or respect, to the rising sun, wash laundry or take a morning dip in the river.

025

FIND THE SOUL OF CORSICA AT CORTE CITADELLE

FRANCE Stacked up the side of a wedge-shaped crag against a spectacular backdrop of granite mountains, Corte epitomizes *l'âme corse*, or "Corsican soul" – a small town marooned amid a grandiose landscape, where a spirit of dogged patriotism is never far from the surface. Corte has been the home of Corsican nationalism since the first National Constitution was drawn up here in 1731, and it remains self-consciously insular. However, the presence of the island's only university lightens the atmosphere noticeably during term time, when the bars and cafés fill with students. For the outsider, Corte's charm is concentrated in the tranquil *haute ville*, where the forbidding *citadelle* presides over a warren of narrow, cobbled streets. The best views are of the town from a distance as dawn breaks over the landscape.

026

TAKE AN EARLY-MORNING CYCLE ON DON KHONG

LAOS Don Khong is surprisingly wide for a river island, and is known locally for its venerable collection of Buddhist temples, some with visible signs of a history stretching back to the sixth or seventh centuries. These, together with the island's good-value accommodation and interesting cuisine, based on fresh fish from the Mekong, make Don Khong the perfect place for indulging both adventurous and lazy moods. The best way to explore Don Khong and experience the traditional sights and sounds of riverside living is to rent a bicycle from one of the guesthouses and set off along the road that circles the island. Get up first thing to witness the sun glistening gold over the Mekong.

027

WATCH DAYBREAK AT THE EDGE OF THE AMAZON

PERU At 3739m above sea level, on the last mountain ridge before the eastern edge of the Amazon forest, the views at Tres Cruces are a marvel at any time: by day you are presented with a vast panorama over the start of a massive cloudforest with all its weird and wonderful vegetation; by night the offering is an enormous star-studded jewel. Arguably, though, the best show is at sunrise, when the natural special effects create a magnificent spectacle. Seen from the highest edge of the Manu Biosphere Reserve, the sunrise is stunning, particularly around the southern hemisphere's winter solstice in June: multicoloured, it's an incredible light show that lasts for hours.

028

REDISCOVER MONUMENT VALLEY

USA The ultimate widescreen landscape, Monument Valley has formed a backdrop to countless Hollywood classics from John Ford's *The Searchers* to Ridley Scott's *Thelma & Louise*. Harshly alluring, the valley – which straddles the Arizona–Utah state line – boasts perfectly distilled Wild West scenery: stark sandstone buttes and forbidding pinnacles of rock that poke out from an endless expanse of drifting red sands. The sheer majesty of the place will take your breath away, but if after seeing all the movies it feels a bit too familiar, a dawn tour can show the area in a new light. As day breaks the scene is transformed; as the sun rises, the 400m-high sandstone turrets, dramatic buttes and massive mesas pose anew as brooding shadows set against a crimson-washed sky.

DAYTIME

There are countless ways to fill your day: get face-to-face with mountain gorillas in the forests of Rwanda, climb strange clusters of boulders in Joshua Tree National Park, or go wild with the locals at Buñol's tomato-throwing festival.

029

SHAKE YOUR THING AT THE NOTTING HILL CARNIVAL

ENGLAND Catch the carnival in Notting Hill, and you'll see the area transformed with a wash of colour, sound, movement and the pure, unadulterated joy that makes this the party highlight of London's festival calendar. On Sunday morning, sound-system guys wire up their towering stacks of speakers, while fragrant smoke wafts from the stalls of early-bird jerk chicken chefs. And then a bass line trembles through the morning air, and trains begin to disgorge crowds of revellers brandishing whistles and horns. The route becomes a seething throng of floats and flags, sequins and feathers, with crowds dancing up a storm to the tunes bouncing from parading trucks of costumed bands. For the next two days, the only thing that matters is the delicious, anarchic freedom of dancing on the streets of London.

030

WITNESS THE ROAR OF VICTORIA FALLS

ZIMBABWE/ZAMBIA Along with Mount Everest and the Grand Canyon, Victoria Falls – or Mosi-oa-Tunya ("the smoke that thunders") – ranks as one of the world's seven natural wonders. No matter how many pictures you've seen beforehand, nothing can prepare you for the awe-inspiring sight and deafening sound of the world's widest curtain of water as it crashes down a huge precipice, producing clouds of spray visible from afar, then squeezes into a zigzag of sheer-sided gorges as a torrent of turbulent rapids carving its way to the Indian Ocean, well over 1000km away. A must-see destination in its own right, its location between Zimbabwe and Zambia, and within reach of Botswana and Namibia, also makes it an ideal springboard for adventures further afield.

031

WATCH A MASKED DANCE IN HAHOE FOLK VILLAGE

SOUTH KOREA Despite its rapid economic growth, South Korea's pastoral traditions are alive and well – nowhere more so than in the country's preserved folk villages. While some exist purely for show, others are functioning communities where life dawdles on at an intentionally slow pace, the residents surviving on a curious mix of home-grown vegetables, government subsidy and tourist-generated income. Hahoe Folk Village is one of the best and most popular in the country, a charming tangle of over a hundred countryside houses nestling in the gentle embrace of an idle river. On your visit, don't miss a performance of Hahoe Pyolshingut Talnori, an age-old masked dance which the government has designated Important Intangible Cultural Asset #69.

032

EXPERIENCE THE RUSH HOUR IN MUMBAI

INDIA Squeeze onto a carriage of the suburban rail network in Mumbai and experience one of the busiest railways on the planet. No other line carries as many passengers, nor crams them into such limited space. The busiest stretch transports nearly 900 million people per year, and at peak times as many as 4700 people may be jammed into a nine-carriage train, resulting in what the rail company, in typically jaunty Mumbai style, refers to as "Super-dense Crush Load". Once on board, you'll realise that not everyone actually occupies floor space: ten percent will be dangling precariously out of the doors. It's worth watching out for the spectacular stream of colour that flows from the "Women-only Carriage" when its female commuters rush onto the platform.

033

TAKE A ROADSIDE SEAT AT THE GIRO D'ITALIA

ITALY Sport isn't the first thing that comes to mind when you think of Italy. But as well as having a passion for football, Italians are crazy about cycling. Visit in May or early June, when the yearly Giro d'Italia, the country's professional cycling race, is held. Find a spot along the route of the race, which is lined with ardent *tifosi* (fans), or follow the progress of the riders on TV screens across the country. The ultimate prize is the *maglia rosa* (pink jersey), while the *maglia verde* (green jersey) is awarded to the "King of the Mountains", the individual winner of each of the mountain stages. If you fancy a less arduous two-wheeled exploration of Italy, take the cypress-lined back roads in Tuscany, or discover the rocky and wild landscape of Sardinia.

034

GET ROMANTIC IN THE ENGLISH LAKE DISTRICT

ENGLAND The Lake District – wild, craggy and epic in scale – has a unique hold on British hearts. From the time of Wordsworth and Coleridge onwards, it has appealed to that part of the nation's character that sees nothing more romantic than a windswept hike up a challenging grassy hill. Catbells, high above the western shore of Derwentwater, has sweeping views of the verdant countryside of this damp northwestern corner of England. From Hawes End, a pier on Derwentwater, you can hike up the sharply ascending path to the top of Catbells; it's a steep scramble, but one that is certainly worth the effort as it rewards you with a panorama of grand dimensions. After the climb, go and relax with a pint in a cosy country pub.

035

SEE ELEPHANTS UNDER THE INFLUENCE

GABON If you're new to safaris and keen to find the quickest, easiest route to a plain teeming with zebras, lions and giraffes, then Loango isn't for you. But if you're prepared to a endure a long journey for a wildlife-watching experience that's unlike anything else Africa has to offer, it might be your kind of place. Loango's unusual juxtaposition of habitats, including undeveloped beach, savannahs and forest, makes it an outstanding place to visit. Forest elephants, which are daintier than their better-known cousins, are partial to a hallucinogenic root, ibago, which grows wild in Loango's forests. If, as your guide drives you around the park, you come across an elephant that's under the influence, you could be in for a close encounter.

036

FEAST YOUR EYES AT A MOROCCAN TANNERY

MOROCCO There is a compulsive fascination about the tanneries Chouwara, the biggest in Fez and the most striking sight in the Medina. Every morning, when the tanneries are at their most active, you can watch from shop balconies as an unbelievably Gothic fantasy is enacted, with tanners treating hides amid vats containing dye and pigeon dung, while hundreds of skins lie spread out on nearby rooftops to dry. The rotation of colours in the honeycombed vats follows a traditional sequence – yellow (supposedly "saffron", but in fact turmeric), red (poppy), blue (indigo), green (mint) and black (antimony).

037
SHOP FOR TRINKETS IN TOKYO

JAPAN For centuries now, the approach to Sensō-ji, Tokyo's oldest temple, has been lined with colourful shops. In the beginning they served religious men, weary from months on the road, but now they cater for pilgrims of a very different kind. Clamber up from the subway and out onto the streets of ancient Asakusa, dodging geishas, smog and rickshaws, to join the thousands of tourists swarming around the vast paper lantern that swings from Kaminarimon ("Thunder Gate"). From here, enter Nakamise-dōri, a 200m-long shopping street that sparkles with polythene-wrapped gifts. At the far end of the thoroughfare, you'll find an enormous black cauldron chugging incense into the sky, drawing new worshippers to the temple and bestowing health on those already there.

038
ADMIRE THE VATICAN MUSEUMS

ITALY The Vatican Museums amount to the largest, richest, most compelling and perhaps most exhausting collection of art in the world: a set of museums so stuffed with antiquities that they put most other European collections to shame. The queues that snake around the Vatican walls are almost legendary; however, standing and wilting under a relentless Roman sun for hours on end before stepping into the museums' hallowed coolness is all part of the experience. Once in the Vatican, you have a choice of routes, so decide how long you want to spend inside, and what you want to see, before you start exploring. Take a day-long trek round the 7km of galleries or, if time is tight, squeeze in a flying visit to the stunning Sistine Chapel adorned with Michelangelo's magnificent ceiling and wall frescoes.

039

PULL ON YOUR BOOTS IN CORSICA

FRANCE The three-hour walk from Col de la Croix to
Girolata is a popular hike: the trail hugs the headland,
revealing ever more impressive views of the Scandola
marine reserve, until you catch your first glimpse of the
tiny fishing haven set against the vivid red cliffs behind.
Girolata's short stretch of stony beach and few houses are
dominated by a stately seventeenth-century watchtower,
and for most of the year this is one of the most idyllic
spots on the island. From June to September, though,
daily boat trips from Porto and Calvi ensure the village is
swamped during the middle of the day, so if you want to
make the most of the scenery and peace and quiet, walk
here and stay a night in one of the *gîtes*.

040

BROWSE ANTIQUES IN BEIJING

CHINA There's no shortage of antique stores and markets in China's capital, offering opium pipes, jade statues, porcelain Mao figurines, mahjong sets, Red Guard alarm clocks, Fu Manchu glasses, and all manner of bric-a-brac – pretty much all of it fake. The jade is actually soapstone, inset jewels are glass, and that venerable painting is a print stained with tea. So long as you're not browsing for heirlooms, Panjiayuan – also called the "Dirt Market" – is a good place to head, with a vast range of souvenirs and secondhand goods for sale; among the junk, you'll find decently priced traditional souvenirs such as seals, kites, papercuts (images cut into thin card), tea sets and ornamental chopsticks.

041

SIP COFFEE IN AMSTERDAM

THE NETHERLANDS The Dutch concept of *gezellig* doesn't translate easily. It's a cocktail of cosiness, friendliness, informal acceptance and companionship, and sums up the special ethos of the city perfectly. A lingering summer picnic in the Vondelpark; a rainy afternoon spent in one of Amsterdam's coffee shops with friends and a plateful of chocolate-chip-and-hash cookies; watching ice-skaters on the frozen canals under twinkling lights; sampling some of the Netherlands' finest pilsners in a *bruin* café (so called because years of smoke and spilled beer have stained these typical Dutch drinking holes a characteristic brown); and of course sipping coffee in one of the many speciality cafés that have popped up all across Amsterdam and offer perfectly crafted coffee made from the very best quality beans.

042

EXPLORE INDIA'S MOST COLOURFUL CITY

INDIA Tamil Nadu – India's Hindu heartland – boasts a tradition of magnificent architecture, with towering gateways dominating towns whose temple complexes remain the focus of everyday life. Of all of them, Madurai – one of the subcontinent's oldest cities – is the most stunning. Your days can be filled wandering the streets – many complete with their own roaming cows – haggling in the market and exploring the Sri Meenakshi-Sundareshwarar temple. This vast complex, boasting massive *gopuras* writhing with multicoloured mythological figures and crowned by golden finials, remains the greatest man-made spectacle of the south. Every day there are 15,000 visitors, and on Fridays numbers reach more than 25,000, while the temple's ritual life spills out into the streets in a ceaseless round of processions.

043

REACH FOR THE SKIES IN THE SAVINJA ALPS

SLOVENIA Cutting through the Savinja Alps near the Austrian border, Logarska Dolina is Slovenia's most impressive alpine glacial valley. Rolling expanses of green meadows and pastures are bordered by tall, pine-blanketed mountains, with an enormous grey cliff face bearing down from the southern end. There's a wealth of sports and activities to keep you occupied and daredevils can take to the skies from the Panoramic Road, which snakes along the side of the valley. Buckle yourself into a harness with the pilot and launch from the side of the mountain to soar like a bird over trees, small scatterings of farm houses and a lone church.

044

FIND THE FRESHEST PRODUCE IN VENICE

ITALY Venice is notoriously one of the world's most expensive cities to visit – but it's also one of the priciest to live in. Anything on sale in a Venetian shop is likely to have arrived there in three stages: by lorry to the docks; then by barge or motorboat to the canalside nearest to the shop; and then by hand-barrow to the doorway, a procedure that often involves hauling the load over several bridges. Every leg of the journey, of course, adds a mark-up to the price the customer pays. For something different, visit the San Barnaba grocery barge, moored near the Ponte dei Pugni, which cuts out the middleman and is a traditional place to pick up fruit and vegetables.

045

TRY THE LIFE AQUATIC IN THE RED SEA

EGYPT Over the last 25 years Hurghada has been transformed from a fishing village into a booming town of around 180,000 people. This phenomenal growth is almost entirely due to tourism, and it was diving – some of the best in Egypt – that really put the town on the map. And it does big business: Hurghada welcomes hordes of tourists each week, and has more than a thousand tour boats. There are more coral islands here than reefs, including about ten islands within day-trip range and many more amazing sites that can be visited on extended dive safaris or live-aboards. Come and dive here and you can enjoy an abundance of marine life, and in deeper waters get the chance to see lurker sharks, giant moray eels and manta rays.

046

WATCH A GAME OF KATAW

LAOS The country's most popular traditional sport, Kataw, is an ancient, hands-free hotchpotch of volleyball, tennis and football – and it calls for some serious aerial acrobatics. The main aim is to keep the woven rattan ball off the floor, but chests, heads and legs can all be used, so there's plenty of room for flamboyant mid-air strikes. Kataw originally made its way to Laos from the Sultanate of Malacca more than 500 years ago and has gone on to become something of a national obsession: matches take place everywhere from the banks of the Mekong River to inner-city schoolyards. When you see one in action, return the players' welcoming smiles and it'll be only a matter of time before you're invited to step up to the net.

047

EXPLORE GUATEMALA'S JUNGLE PARADISE

GUATEMALA If you are a wildlife-lover then Guatemala should be high on your list of must-visit destinations. This small country in Central America has an incredibly diverse ecosystem with a dramatic and wildly beautiful landscape, particularly in the unique lowlands of the vast northern department of Petén, which occupies about a third of Guatemala but contains just over three percent of the country's population. This expanse of tropical rainforest, swamp and savannah stretches into southern Mexico and across the Maya Mountains to Belize, and huge tracts remain virtually untouched. Ancient mahogany trees tower 50m above the forest floor, sheltering an extraordinarily rich variety of wildlife – hummingbirds, toucans, buzzards, wild turkeys and birds of paradise, and, beneath the forest canopy, lumbering tapir, ocelots, deer, coatis and jaguars. Sadly, this jungle paradise is under threat; despite the fact that forty percent of the department is officially protected by the Maya Biosphere Reserve, waves of settlers have cleared enormous sections, and oil exploration and commercial logging have brought with them mountains of money and machinery, cutting new roads deep into the forest. Organizations such as UNESCO are attempting to halt the destruction of the rainforest, and you can do your bit by booking with a tour operator that has a focus on the preservation and conservation of Guatemala. The forests and swamps of the Mirador Basin at the core of the reserve are still well preserved and have been spared, thanks to the efforts of environmental campaigners.

048

VISIT CHILE'S LAST SURVIVING STILT VILLAGE

CHILE Built at the head of a 20km fjord on Chiloé Island, Castro has had its fair share of difficulties; struck several times by natural disasters since the first recorded earthquake in 1646, most of its old town has been burned, knocked down or washed away. Built as it was almost entirely of back-to-back wooden buildings, Castro of the 1930s was a fire waiting to happen. In 1936 when catastrophe hit, all the inhabitants could do was head for the sea, where they watched their homes burn from the waters of the icy fjord. Miraculously, some buildings survived and today you can see groups of brightly coloured *palafitos* (houses on stilts) on the waterfront. The last remaining such structures in the country, the local government is torn between preserving them as national monuments and condemning them as insanitary slums.

049

SEE A SNAPSHOT OF ROMAN LIFE IN POMPEII

ITALY Some two thousand citizens perished in the 79AD eruption of Vesuvius, asphyxiated by toxic fumes, their homes buried beneath volcanic ash and pumice. Pompeii is a remarkable record of a town stopped in its tracks, and a visit here gives an insight into the lives of ordinary ancient Romans. Coach-loads of sightseers pound Pompeii's ancient cobblestones every day, photographing its chipped mosaics and fading frescoes, trooping around the remains of its elegant villas and sniggering at the erotic art in its ancient brothel. But Pompeii is now at risk of eradication for a second time; centuries of foot traffic and the ravages of the elements are taking their toll. Such is the danger that in 2013 a massive €90 million restoration project got under way.

050

GET DRENCHED UNDER NIAGARA FALLS

USA/CANADA Every second, almost three-quarters of a million gallons of water explode over the Niagara Falls, with boats, walkways, observation towers and helicopters all conspiring to get you as close as possible to this natural spectacle. These methods cannot compete, of course, with the feats of tightrope walker Blondin, who crossed the falls repeatedly in the 1890s (sometimes with passengers on his back), nor with those daredevils who've taken the plunge in barrels; remarkably, ten of the fifteen survived. In winter the falls freeze into gigantic, razor-tipped icicles, while at night the whole scene is lit up, and the coloured waters tumble dramatically into blackness. The classic way to experience Niagara is on the *Maid of the Mist* ferry, which has been carrying passengers through the dense, drenching spray since 1846.

051

RIDE BATTAMBANG'S BAMBOO TRAIN

CAMBODIA If you're in Battambang don't miss the chance to ride the *norry*, a quirky railway that runs along a section of track just outside the city. A local answer to the lack of scheduled train services in Cambodia, the "bamboo train" shuttles people, rice and livestock back and forth upon wooden platforms, which are placed on top of a wheeled metal carriage powered by a small engine. During the thirty-minute trip these "cars" at times reach 40km/hr, crashing through jungle undergrowth, rattling over little bridges and whizzing past rice paddies. Meeting another car on the track travelling in the opposite direction is an event in itself: the one with the fewest passengers has to be dismantled and cleared to the side to allow the other to pass – an impressively swift operation.

052

EXPERIENCE PUERTO RICO'S OLDEST CARNAVAL

PUERTO RICO Ponce holds Puerto Rico's oldest and most dazzling Carnaval, opening with a procession led by King Momo (the traditional "King of Carnivals") and figures known as *vejigantes*, mostly local boys whose ornate masks are embellished with outlandish colours and devilish horns. The original purpose was to scare people – the *vejigantes* traditionally represented Moorish warriors – and these days you'll see them merrily thwacking the kids who line the streets with a *vejiga*, a dried cow's bladder blown up like a balloon. The merrymaking ends on Shrove Tuesday with the bizarre *Entierro de la Sardina* (Burial of the Sardine), a mock funeral procession attended by hyperbolic cries and wails from everyone in sight. A fish is symbolically burnt at the climax, signifying the purging of sins before the beginning of Lent.

053

GET YOUR KICKS ON ROUTE 66

USA Some ninety years since it was completed, eighty since John Steinbeck called it "the mother road, the road of flight" in *The Grapes of Wrath*, and seventy since Bobby Troup set it all down in rhyme, Route 66 remains one of the most seductive reasons to visit Southwest USA. Quickly superseded by freeways, the road's heyday as the nation's premier cross-country route – winding from Chicago to LA – lasted barely twenty years. Nonetheless, substantial stretches survive, complete with the motels and drive-ins that became icons of vernacular American architecture. Today, Harley-Davidsons and restored 1950s roadsters still cruise towns such as Albuquerque and Flagstaff, before disappearing into the route's empty desertscapes, such as those between Grants and Gallup in New Mexico, or Seligman and Kingman in Arizona.

054

EXPLORE CHEFCHAOUEN'S BRIGHT BLUE MEDINA

MOROCCO Getting lost in Chefchaouen's narrow and uncrowded streets is a photographer's dream, with stray cats posing in front of ornate turquoise doorways and impossibly old men shuffling up and down blue staircases in conical hooded cloaks. There are aspects of the old town that make you feel like you could have travelled back in time: the *furn*, or communal bakery, still delivers warm, circular loaves of bread to locals every morning, while on market day hunched-over women descend from the mountain farms to sell vats of milk. It is only when you peek into a dark room full of kids gathered around a games console, or pass a carpet store blasting out Bruno Mars, that you will be politely reminded of the century you're in.

055

CELEBRATE OKTOBERFEST IN MUNICH

GERMANY Few days come more merry than those spent at Oktoberfest, Munich's legendary beer festival which, despite its name, is generally held during the last two weeks in September. The first Oktoberfest was in October – in 1810 – but over time the festival has got longer and the dates have shifted forward. Predictably enough, massive and widespread public drunkenness is a regular phenomenon – some seven million visitors manage to down over four million litres of beer in just sixteen days – which doesn't stop the revellers from visiting the enormous funfair that runs alongside the beer tents. One additional annual ritual is the intake of breath at the price of a *Mass* (litre) of beer – it may be good, but carousing Oktoberfest-style certainly doesn't come cheap.

056

FALL FOR FOOTBALL IN LA BOCA

ARGENTINA If you've ever wondered why Argentina punches above its weight in international football, a wander through Buenos Aires' poorer *barrios* should offer a few clues. Everywhere you go you'll see street walls plastered with football slogans and people kicking a ball about. Match days are all-consuming: the city talks of nothing else, and while a game is on, daily life comes to a halt – nowhere more so than in La Boca, home to Argentina's most popular and most famous team. If you can, bag a ticket for a match at the intensely compact La Bombonera stadium, and join the mass of Boca Juniors' supporters, fans so dedicated that their football obsession can even follow them to the grave in the club's own blue-and-yellow-garlanded cemetery.

057

TAKE A LEAP OF FAITH IN THE COSTA RICAN RAINFOREST

COSTA RICA Winding its way north to the border with Nicaragua, the languid Río Colorado snakes around coffee plantations, skirts volcanoes and cuts through thick jungle buzzing with toucans and monkeys. Near the tiny town of Llano del Rosario, it ebbs under the rusted steel girders of the old Río Colorado Bridge – at 70m, one of the highest bungee bridges in the Americas, and a quite gorgeous place to take the plunge. The essence of bungee jumping has changed little since the people of Pentecost Island in Vanuatu first strapped vines to their ankles and hurled themselves off specially built wooden towers. It's a simple business really: all you have to do is hold your nerve, then let yourself drop at dizzying speed through the forest canopy towards the waters below. Easy.

058

ADMIRE MOROCCO'S MOST EXQUISITE BUILDING

MOROCCO If there is just one building you should seek out in Fez – or, not to put too fine a point on it, in Morocco – it's the Medersa Bou Inania. The most elaborate, extravagant and beautiful of all Merenid monuments, it comes close to perfection in every aspect of its construction: carved dark cedar, classic zellij tilework, and striking stucco work. You enter via the exquisite marble courtyard, the medersa's outstanding feature, where the decoration covers every possible surface. Cedar beams ring three sides of the courtyard and a sash of elegant black Kufic script wraps around four sides, dividing the zellij from the stucco; unusually, it comprises a list of the properties whose incomes were given as an endowment, rather than the standard Koranic inscriptions.

059

GET SOME PERSPECTIVE AT SOUTH INDIA'S HOLIEST SITE

INDIA Hindus tend to be followers of either Vishnu or Shiva, but the sacred island of Rameshwaram brings the two together, as this is where the god Rama – an incarnation of Vishnu – worshipped Shiva in the Ramayana. One of South India's holiest pilgrimage sites, the Rameshwaram temple is distinctive for its corridors, with their extreme length (205m, flanked by 1212 massive pillars) giving a remarkable impression of receding perspective. Before entering the inner sections, pilgrims bathe at each of the 22 *tirthas* (tanks) in the temple – hence the groups of dripping-wet pilgrims, most of them fully clothed, that you may see. Each *tirtha* is said to have special benefits, with relief from debt, wisdom and long life among them.

060

DISCOVER KERALA'S UNIQUE MARTIAL ART

INDIA Practised in special, earth-floored gyms and pits across the state, *kalarippayattu* is Kerala's unique martial art – a brand of acrobatic combat that draws heavily on yoga and ancient Indian knowledge of the human body. The bodyguards of medieval warlords and chieftains formalized it in the twelfth century, but its origins are believed to stretch back two thousand years or more. Students are taught a complex set of exercises designed to render their bodies strong and flexible: kicks, jumps, animal postures, spins, step sequences and stretches, joined in increasingly complicated patterns. Once they've mastered the set moves, students are eventually introduced to combat with various weapons, including swords and spears. The final stage, *verum kaythari*, focuses on bare-handed fighting against an armed enemy.

061

LOSE YOURSELF IN COASTAL CONNEMARA

IRELAND On the far western edge of Europe, the starkly beautiful region of Connemara is a great place to get lost. Cut off from the rest of Ireland by the 25-mile barrier of Lough Corrib, the lie of the land at first looks simple, with two statuesque mountain ranges, the Maam Turks and the Twelve Bens, bordered by the deep fjord of Killary Harbour to the north. The coast, however, is full of jinks and tricks, a hopeless maze of inlets, peninsulas and small islands. Dozens of sparkling lakes and vast blanket bogs covered in purple moor grass further blur the distinction between land and water. Throw in a fickle climate, which can turn from blazing sunshine to soaking mist in seconds, and the carefree sense of disorientation is complete.

062

ENJOY A DAY AT THE DESERT RACES

DUBAI Despite the city-state's rapid expansion, the district of Nad Al Sheba in Dubai is still largely untouched desert, shifting dunes where the area's Bedouin people once eked out an existence, hunting with falcons and dogs – called *saluki* – which could outrun and bring down desert hares. Nowadays the district is home to one of Dubai's quirkier attractions: the Camel Racecourse. Races are held here from about 7am during the winter months, but even if no events are scheduled, you can come and watch the animals being exercised early in the morning. It's a captivating sight: literally hundreds of colourfully dressed beasts and their heavily robed riders amble – and occasionally gallop – across the desert, while their owners charge after them in 4WDs shrieking encouragement.

063

WATCH FISHERMEN AT WORK ON THE MEKONG RIVER

LAOS As the Mekong River streams down through southern Laos on its 4184km journey from the Tibetan plateau to its south Vietnam delta, the terrain flattens. Braiding out across vast wetlands, the river creates a landlocked archipelago of "Four Thousand Islands": Si Phan Don. While the region is a playground for Southeast Asia's few surviving freshwater Irrawaddy dolphins, it's sheer heaven for fishermen, with islanders hurling nets off slippery rocks and balancing on bamboo scaffolds above whirlpools. Their catch ends up variously as *lap pa*, a salad of raw fish minced up with garlic, chillies and shallots; *pa dek*, a thick, fermented fish sauce that goes with everything; and the local speciality, *mok pa*, an aromatic parcel of fish steamed in banana leaves.

064

SAMPLE FOOD FROM AROUND THE WORLD AT BOROUGH MARKET

ENGLAND From the vintage stores and food stalls of Brick Lane to the floral abundance of Columbia Road, London's East End markets could fill a weekend of browsing and bargain-hunting. But for the best foodie shopping in London, head to Borough Market, which is tucked beneath the railway arches between Borough High Street and Southwark Cathedral. The early-morning wholesale fruit and vegetable market winds up around 8am and is one of the few still trading under its original Victorian wrought-iron shed. It's very popular, so get there early on Friday and Saturday to sample dishes from the busy specialist food market, with stalls selling top-quality and pricey produce from around the world, or visit on a Wednesday or Thursday when it's less busy.

VARIETY: Blood Oranges
COUNTRY: Italy
PRICE: 1-80 kg

065

TRAVEL BY CHICKEN BUS IN GUATEMALA

GUATEMALA Virtually everyone takes the chicken bus in Guatemala. Easily distinguished by their trademark clouds of thick, black fumes, these buses – also known as *camionetas* – originally ferried North American children to and from school. Once they move down to these parts, they're decked out with gaudy "go-faster" stripes and windshield stickers bearing religious mantras. Comfort, however, is not customizable: there's little legroom and no air-con, while drivers tend to have a fixation for speed and overtaking on blind corners. The drivers' helpers (*ayundantes*), meanwhile, are generally overworked and underage, constantly scrambling up to the roof to retrieve bags, collecting fares and bellowing out destinations. Travel by chicken bus may be uncomfortable, but it's certainly never dull.

066

HANG OUT WITH PENGUINS AT BOULDERS BEACH

SOUTH AFRICA Think of penguins and icy landscapes inevitably spring to mind. Yet these "flippant yet dignified" birds (to quote Allen Lane who used them as a logo on his paperbacks) can be found as far north as the semi-tropical Galápagos Islands. On family-friendly Boulders Beach, close to Cape Town, you can actually swim among them. Seeing them is easy – just get out of your car at the Boulders Beach car park, half an hour's drive from Central Cape Town, and there they are, sunning themselves on the great granite rocks that give the beach its name, or walking around on the beach itself. Don't expect companionship as you swim in the calm, clear Atlantic waters though. The penguins don't hang around, instead they streak past at up to 25km/hr to fish in the waters way off the coast.

067

HAVE YOUR SHOES SHINED IN CIEGO DE ÁVILA

CUBA Private enterprise in Cuba, with all the strict rules and regulations that govern it, expresses itself in some pretty novel ways. Small-scale businesses, whose impact on state control of the economy is all but insignificant, have flourished in the jamboree of street-side vendors found in neighbourhoods and cities – such as the modest and unaffected urban centre of Ciego de Ávila in the heart of the island. The most common are the front-room caterers, the Cuban answer to the local candy store or mobile café, churning out everything from cakes and peanut bars to pizzas and sandwiches. Understanding the need to extend the life of replaceable items, enterprising businesspeople have developed roaring trades in cigarette lighter refuelling, watch mending and shoe cleaning.

068

GO WILDLIFE WATCHING IN ETOSHA NATIONAL PARK

NAMIBIA A country of vast open landscapes and an array of natural wonders, Namibia promises adventure. While tourists have traditionally been drawn to Namibia for its landscapes, the country is now also attracting attention for its wildlife; specifically the increasing numbers of rare large mammals that are thriving here. Beyond the game-rich confines of Etosha – Namibia's premier national park, teeming with beasts like the Thomson's gazelle – the world's largest concentrations of free-roaming cheetah stalk the plains, while desert-adapted elephant and black rhino lumber along the valleys of northwest Namibia. In many cases these animals are protected by local communities working hand in hand with conservationists.

069

DISCOVER COWBOY CULTURE AT A CHILEAN RODEO

CHILE If you're in the Central Valley between September and April don't miss the chance to see a Chilean rodeo in its birthplace. The season kicks off on Independence Day, September 18, with regional competitions eliminating all but the finest horses and *huasos*, who go on to the national championships in Rancagua in April. Rodeos are performed in crescent-shaped stadiums called *medialunas* ("half moons"). The participants are *huasos* – cowboys, or horsemen – who cut a dashing figure with their bright, finely woven ponchos, broad-rimmed hats, carved wooden stirrups and shining silver spurs. And there's more than just watching the action in the stadium; competitions fill the weekend and are a great chance to sample regional food, gourmet wine and the sweet fruity alcohol known as *chicha* – and to join in with the dancing.

070

RELAX ON VARADERO BEACH

CUBA Varadero is *the* package resort in Cuba, a giant playground of large-scale resort hotels spread across a 25km-long peninsula that protrudes like a fingertip from the north coast of the island. The golden carpet of fine sand bathed by placid emerald-green waters is almost the perfect vision of a tropical paradise; indeed, before the Revolution, this was one of the most renowned, modern and hedonistic holiday spots in the Caribbean. Castro's hostility to tourism changed much of that, but things have been on the upswing since the 1990s. Despite the signs of burgeoning tourism – from the spread of luxury hotels to the hawkers peddling souvenirs on the beach – a lingering legacy of peeling shopfronts and down-at-heel restaurants and clubs keeps Varadero peculiarly and defiantly Cuban.

071
SURF MALOLO BARRIER REEF

FIJI This South Pacific paradise hosts a number of international surfing competitions, and no one who's serious about the sport can resist Fiji's powerful reef breaks and consistent, world-class waves. The dozen or so breaks along the 30km length of the Malolo Barrier Reef are accessible from Momi Bay or Uciwai on Fiji's main island, or Namotu Island Resort a few kilometres southwest. Conditions are at their most challenging between April and November, and less experienced surfers are advised to consider the summer months instead, when swells are smaller and winds lighter. Keep in mind that although Fiji's vibrant coral reefs are astonishingly beautiful, reef breaks on Manolo are shallow and wipeout is likely to be painful.

072

CLIMB THE GREAT WALL OF CHINA

CHINA The Great Wall is one of those sights that you've seen and heard so much about that you know reality is going to have a tough time living up to the hype. But having made it all the way to Beijing, it seems perverse to ignore this overblown landmark, so arm yourself with a thermos of tea and catch a bus north from the capital to Simatai, one of several sections of this 4800km-long structure which has been restored. Not even swarms of hawkers and crowds of tourists can ruin the sight of this blue-grey ribbon snaking across the dusty, shattered hills into the hazy distance, beyond which one end finally runs into the sea and the other simply stops in northwestern China's deserts.

073

SHOP AT ST-OUEN FLEA MARKET

FRANCE It's easy to lose track of an entire morning browsing the acres of fine antiques, covetable curios and general odds and ends at St-Ouen, the mother of Paris's flea markets. It's come a long way from the days when secondhand mattresses, clothes and other infested junk were sold here in a free-for-all zone outside the city walls. Nowadays, it's predominantly a proper – and very expensive – antiques market, with over a dozen separate sections covering some two thousand shops. To better your chances of finding something you could feasibly carry home, head for Marché Vernaison, the oldest in the complex, and the closest thing to a real flea market. Its maze-like, creeper-covered alleys are fun to wander along, threading your way between stalls selling all manner of bric-a-brac.

074

EXPLORE FRANZ JOSEF AND FOX GLACIERS

NEW ZEALAND On the west coast of New Zealand's South Island, two gleaming white rivers of ice force their way down towards the thick rainforest of the coastal plain, forming a palpable connection between the coast and the highest alpine peaks. As Maori legend has it, a beautiful girl named Hinehukatere loved walking in the mountains so much that she encouraged her lover, Tawe, to climb alongside her. He slipped and fell to his death, and Hinehukatere cried so copiously that her tears formed glaciers. Now going by the somewhat less poetic monikers of Franz Josef and Fox, these are two of the largest and most impressive of the sixty-odd glaciers that creak off the South Island's icy backbone, together forming the centrepiece of the rugged Westland National Park.

075

WITNESS THE NARROW CANALS OF GHENT

BELGIUM Ghent's beauty may be eclipsed by that of its ancient rival, Bruges, but it still musters some superb Gothic buildings and a bevy of delightful, intimate streetscapes, where its distinctive brick houses are woven around a skein of narrow canals. The atmosphere here is markedly different from that of its neighbour, however, with the tourist industry supplementing, rather than dominating, the local economy. As a consequence, Ghent preserves the raw and authentic edges that Bruges has tried so hard to iron out, and its busy centre reflects the city's ancient class and linguistic divide: head to the streets south of the Korenmarkt to discover elegant old mansions, while to the north, Flemish Ghent is all narrow alleys and low brick houses.

076

THROW TOMATOES AT THE LOCALS IN BUÑOL

SPAIN La Tomatina – Buñol's tomato-throwing festival – is about as wild as Spanish fiestas get, and is an event not to be missed. For one day in late August around 30,000 people and a fleet of trucks carrying 120,000 tonnes of tomatoes descend on the small town. For one hour madness breaks out as truckers hurl the ripe, pulpy fruit at the crowd, who in turn throw the pulp back at the trucks, at each other, in the air – everywhere. At 1pm, an explosion signals the end of the battle and the local fire brigade arrives to hose down the combatants, buildings and streets. And then, miraculously, within the hour, everyone arrives back on the street, perfectly turned out, to enjoy the rest of the fiesta.

077

SAVOUR THE SAV IN MARLBOROUGH'S VINEYARDS

NEW ZEALAND When Marlborough's Cloudy Bay Sauvignon Blanc hit the international wine shelves in the late 1980s its zingy fruitiness got jaded tongues wagging. All of a sudden New Zealand was on the world wine map, with the pin stuck firmly in the north of the South Island. Half a dozen regions now boast significant wine trails, but all roads lead back to Marlborough, still the country's largest grape-growing area, protected by the sheltering hills of the Richmond Range, and blessed with more than 2400 hours of sunshine a year. Cellar doors around the region are gradually becoming more sophisticated, with their own restaurants and specialist food stores, but the emphasis is still mainly on the wine itself. And tasting it. To squeeze the very best from the area, start by visiting Montana Brancott, the biggest and most established operation hereabouts. Take their winery tour to get a feel for how wine is made nowadays, then stick around for a brief lesson on wine appreciation. Even those familiar with the techniques will learn something of the qualities Marlborough winemakers are trying to achieve. Next visit Cloudy Bay. Of course you'll want to try the famous Sav, still drinking well today and available for tasting. Somehow it always seems that little bit fresher and fruitier when sampled at source out of a decent glass. Come lunchtime, head for Highfield Estate with its distinctive Tuscan-style tower and dine in the sun overlooking the vines.

078
TEST YOUR CYCLING NERVES IN THE ITALIAN DOLOMITES

ITALY During the winter months skiers and snowboarders descend on the glamorous resort town of Cortina d'Ampezzo – put on the map after hosting the 1956 Winter Olympics. For the rest of the year it's an increasingly popular base for mountain biking in the UNESCO-protected Dolomites, with a number of "bike hotels" in town offering storage, maintenance and massage therapy for cyclists. The area's many cable cars and chairlifts are kept open over the summer months, giving mountain bikers the luxury to drift to the top of the trails without the burden of ever having to pedal uphill. From the top you may well find yourself above the clouds, riding against the backdrop of the otherworldly, splintering peaks that characterize the range.

079
FOLLOW IN MAYA FOOTSTEPS AT NOHOCH MUL

MEXICO If you had climbed the looming Nohoch Mul twenty years ago, chances are you would have had only monkeys and birds for company. Today, coach tours flood the site of Cobá from the early morning and there's almost always a crowd enjoying the shade at the foot of the pyramid, recovering from the climb or psyching themselves up for the attempt. The pyramid doesn't immediately look that impressive, but start to clamber up the narrow, precipitous and mercilessly shadeless stairway and you will quickly appreciate just how big it is. Once you reach the temple at the top you will be amply rewarded for the climb: taking in nearby lakes as well as jungle stretching uninterrupted to the horizon, the views from up here are nothing short of awe-inspiring.

080

WANDER THE SHORES OF THE BOSPHORUS

TURKEY You could be forgiven for thinking that swimming, tea-drinking and fishing are the Turkish national pastimes; along the shores of the Bosphorus, plenty of hours are unashamedly devoted to the enjoyment of each. Behind Ortaköy's eighteenth-century Büyük Mecidiye Mosque, *Zuma*, an outpost of London's finest Japanese restaurant, competes for custom with a slew of traditional waterfront cafés. Istanbul trendies trawl the nearby boutiques, while rowdy kids beat the heat with a splash around in the Bosphorus – the wide strait demarking the border between Europe and Asia. Atatürk, modern Turkey's founding father, used to dive here too, but strong currents and waters teeming with jellyfish mean that taking the plunge is pretty much for experienced locals only.

081

GORGE ON STREET FOOD IN HUÉ

VIETNAM From hawkers with cauldrons of soup dangling from shoulder poles, to pushcarts, market stalls and makeshift "street kitchens", Vietnam's street-food scene is unsurpassed. Though the choice is enormous, most vendors are highly specialized, serving one type of food or even just a single dish, but they cook it to perfection. One of the best places to spend a day snacking to your heart's content is Hué, which boasts an array of famous speciality foods. Favourites include: *banh khoai*, a crispy fried pancake with pork, shrimp and bean sprouts, served with a peanut and sesame sauce; *bun bo*, a deliciously spicy noodle soup flavoured with beef, shrimp and basil; and to wash it all down, *chè*, a refreshing drink that is made from fruit, lotus seed or a blend of green bean and coconut.

082

EXPLORE ONE OF LAKE GARDA'S PRETTIEST SPOTS

ITALY Lake Garda, Italy's largest lake, acts as a bridge between the Alps and the rest of the country. At the northern end the lake is tightly enclosed by mountains that drop sheer into the water with villages wedged into the cliffs, while to the south, it spreads out, flanked by gentle hills. Undoubtedly one of the prettiest spots to stay is the scenically impressive Sirmione. Only accessed through ancient castle walls, the lovely village squeezes along a long narrow promontory out into the placid waters. Climb the old castle turrets to take in the panoramic views out over the tiled rooftops, turquoise waters of the lake, and distant cypress-clad mountains. Even better, rent a boat and explore the lake yourself – a small island with a lone palace atop is within easy reach.

083

DISCOVER STONE TOWN'S HISTORY

TANZANIA Stone Town's gruesome history as a centre of the slave trade is perhaps best understood by visiting Tippu Tip's House along the poetically named Suicide Alley. Tippu Tip was once the richest and most powerful slave-trader in East Africa, and many a European explorer curried his favour to obtain safe passage on the mainland, as his influence – and fear of his name – spread. Climb the steps to the front door and you'll notice that Tippu Tip's once opulent home is now in an advanced state of decay. Nevertheless, its elaborate door and black-and-white marble steps still set it apart, and the house is currently occupied by various Zanzibari families, evidently undaunted by the popular belief that the house is haunted by the spirits of slaves.

084

CHALLENGE THE LOCALS TO A GAME OF DOMINOES

ST LUCIA All over the Caribbean, in wooden sheds with fresh breezes blowing through, in village rum shops or town squares, locals practise the time-honoured form of killing time, Caribbean-style: a game of dominoes. You'll soon realize that this is not child's play but a serious game for adults, played for money and pride, and with a concentration and energy quite remarkable for a game of such simplicity. You can usually tell when a game is in progress: you'll hear shouting and the clacking of tiles or "bones" being slapped down on the table as players try to intimidate opponents, or the sound of exuberant celebrations. The game that keeps the drowsy island afternoon awake is also played competitively, and the Caribbean is always well represented in world domino championships.

085

CLAMBER UP THE ACTIVE VOLCÁN IRAZÚ

COSTA RICA Famous for having had the gall to erupt on the day President Kennedy visited the country on March 19, 1963, Volcán Irazú has been more or less calm ever since. But while it is less active in terms of bubblings and rumblings than the other volcanoes here, its deep crater and the algae-green lake that fills it create an undeniably dramatic sight. Hike to the top, through the blasted lunar landscape of the Parque Nacional Volcán Irazú, and you'll find a suprising amount of vegetation clinging on to its slopes, making the most of the fertile volcanic soil. You'll also be blessed with the fantastic views all the way to the Caribbean coast.

086

FEEL THE SPLASH OF A HUMPBACK IN HÚSAVÍK

ICELAND The fact that in Icelandic the word for beached whale is the same as that for jackpot or windfall may give you some clue as to how these seaborne beasts are seen by the locals here. Yes, you may well find whale on the menu in restaurants in Iceland – but thanks to a temporary IWC moratorium on whaling back in the 1980s, whalers were forced to seek alternative sources of income and at that point the whale-watching industry was born. Head out to sea and across Skjálfandi Bay from Húsavík on the island's north coast where, if you are lucky, you may be treated to the unforgettable display of a humpback whale leaping out of the water to expose its whole magnificent body.

087

DISCOVER THE LOST WORLD OF PETRA

JORDAN Ever since a Western adventurer stumbled on the site of Petra in 1812, it has fired imaginations, its grandeur and dramatic setting pushing it – like the Pyramids and the Taj Mahal – into the realms of legend. In its Nabatean golden age, Petra was an extravagantly wealthy city, home to tens of thousands of people. Temples and public buildings were built on a grand scale, watercourses flowed to irrigate lush gardens and the natural earth tones of the buildings were tempered by brightly coloured plasterwork. Though many of Petra's grand buildings are now rubbly excavation sites, there's still plenty here to take your breath away – not least the awe-inspiring Monastery with its facade of almost fifty square metres.

088

GET UP CLOSE WITH A MOUNTAIN GORILLA

RWANDA A face-to-face encounter with a mountain gorilla in Rwanda's Volcanoes National Park is one of the most exciting wildlife experiences in Africa. And locating the apes in their misty forest home is part of the thrill, an intense, high-altitude slog that has you navigating steep, muddy slopes for between one and five hours. A guided trek high into the Virunga Volcanoes, which support more than half the world's remaining nine hundred mountain gorillas, begins with a dawn start at the park headquarters in Kinigi. The strenuous ascent is worth every step when you finally look into the liquid brown eyes of one of the magnificent bamboo-munching beasts, whose formidable bulk is complemented by a remarkably peaceable temperament.

089

TRY TAPAS AND SHERRY IN JEREZ

SPAIN Join the people of Jerez as they gather for idle chat in palm-lined plazas, toy with tapas and seek shelter from the sun in shady corners of forgotten squares. They wait for June, when the workers head out into the sea of vineyards surrounding their whitewashed town to plant rows of young vines in the chalky soil to grow the fine dry sherry for which the area is famous. In September, the workers return with sackloads of juicy bunches of grapes to bless, press and leave to ferment until the end of November. The sherry is then aged in oak barrels, dropping – a little at a time – from one barrel down to the next until, after at least three years, the first batch, the light, dry fino, is ready.

090

CONQUER THE MAJESTIC PAMIRS ON FOOT

TAJIKISTAN Standing at a skyscraping crossroads – the Himalaya, Karakorum, Hindu Kush and Tien Shan ranges meet here – the magnificent Pamirs remain one of the most unexplored places on the planet. Known as Bam-i-Dunya ("Roof of the World"), this vast, rugged stretch of Central Asia boasts astounding crested peaks and stretches of undulating fields. Visitors can camp with nomads and ride bareback across the steppe – and hike and climb a unique land. While many of Tajikistan's hundred-odd mountains have never been scaled, you can climb Peak Lenin (also known as Ibn Sina Peak), at 7134m the third-highest mountain in the former Soviet Union. Before you set out, acclimatize yourself culturally by trekking from village to village in the lower altitudes.

091

SOAR ABOVE AFRICA'S AWE-INSPIRING WILDLIFE

TANZANIA/KENYA Once a year, an estimated 1.5 million wildebeest, and hundreds of thousands of zebras, antelope and topi begin the world's largest animal migration. Racing from the withering plains of Tanzania's southern Serengeti, to the undulating grasslands of Kenya's Maasai Mara Game Reserve, this is a hazardous, relentless journey of 800km across racing rivers, lethal lakes and deadly lion country. A hot-air balloon ride is undoubtedly one of the best ways to see this awe-inspiring event. From lift-off at dawn to the (often bumpy) landing, a hot-air balloon provides the perfect roost from which to view the migration. As you sweep over the undulating grasslands, take in the spectacular views below – the galloping mass of beasts reduced to something resembling a teeming ant's nest.

092

DISCOVER THE TREASURES OF SPAIN'S QUIRKIEST MUSEUM

SPAIN Although there's been a settlement at Sanlúcar de Barrameda, on Spain's Cádiz coast, since Roman times, it wasn't until the recapture of the town in 1264 by Alfonso X that it grew to become one of sixteenth-century Spain's leading ports. Columbus sailed from here on his third voyage to the Americas, and it was also from here in 1519 that Magellan set out to circumnavigate the globe. Today, Sanlúcar's maritime pedigree is celebrated in the curious Museo del Mar Caracoles, a bizarre lifetime collection of objects retrieved from the sea by eccentric proprietor Garrido García. Something of a latter-day Long John Silver, Señor García proudly conducts tours around his house/museum – a treasure trove of maritime knick-knacks – with a feral pigeon often perched on one shoulder.

093

FEEL THE EARTH MOVE AT A SUMO WRESTLING BOUT

JAPAN There's something fascinating about sumo, Japan's national sport. The age-old pomp and ceremony that surrounds the titanic clashes between enormous, near-naked wrestlers – from the design of the *dohyō* (the ring in which bouts take place) to the wrestler's slicked-back topknot – give the sport a gravitas completely absent from Western wrestling. Accounts of sumo bouts date back around two thousand years, to when it was a Shinto rite connected with praying for a good harvest. Later, sumo developed into a spectator sport, but the old religious trappings remain: the *gyoji* (referee) wears robes similar to those of a Shinto priest, and above the *dohyō* hangs a thatched roof like those found at shrines. At the

start of a bout the two *rikishi* (wrestlers) wade into the ring, wearing only *mawashi* aprons, which are essentially giant jockstraps. Salt is tossed to purify the ring, and then the *rikishi* hunker down and indulge in the time-honoured ritual of psyching each other out with menacing stares. When ready, each *rikishi* attempts to throw his opponent to the ground or out of the ring using one or more of 82 legitimate techniques. The first to touch the ground with any part of his body other than his feet, or to step out of the *dohyō*, loses. Visit the National Sumo Stadium in Ryōgoku to experience a sumo wrestling tournament first-hand (held here in January, May and September); don't forget to pick up a bento box before you take your seat.

094

VISIT THE NGORONGORO CRATER

TANZANIA Some 2.5 million years ago, the reservoir of magma under an enormous volcano towering over the western flank of the Great Rift Valley emptied itself in a huge explosion, leaving a vacuum that caused the mountain to implode under its own weight. In its wake, it left an enormous 600m-deep crater, its 19km diameter now making it the world's largest unbroken and unfolded caldera. This is Ngorongoro Crater, one of Tanzania's wonders, covering approximately three hundred square kilometres and providing a natural amphitheatre for the wildlife spectacle on its floor. The crater contains 25,000 to 30,000 large mammals, including lions, cheetahs, black rhino, elephants, wildebeest, zebra and gazelle.

095

MARVEL AT THE CHURCH OF THE SAVIOUR ON SPILLED BLOOD

RUSSIA The church of the Saviour on Spilled Blood is one of St Petersburg's most striking landmarks, standing out against the predominantly Baroque and Neoclassical architecture of the rest of the city. The spilled blood was that of Tsar Alexander II, who was assassinated on this spot on March 1, 1881. During the 1930s, the Communists briefly turned the church into a museum celebrating the assassination, after which it was used as a warehouse. Now fully restored, the church is well worth a visit: gaze up at the brightly coloured spires before admiring the stunning interior, which is decorated from floor to ceiling with over 7500 square metres of mosaics – more than any other church in the world.

096

KNOCK BACK A RUM AT THE PELICAN BAR

JAMAICA Jamaica's south coast offers varied pleasures, from gentle beach action at the terminally easy-going Treasure Beach to boat safaris in search of crocodiles and manatees on the Black River. Travel just east of here to the secluded fishing village of Parottee, where, thanks to initiatives by hotels and enterprising locals, visitors are slowly arriving to explore nearby swamplands, go birdwatching, bask on golden-sand beaches and take boat tours to *Pelican Bar* – a ramshackle bird's-nest of a bar built on stilts in the middle of the sea. There are few more tranquil places to sample one of the island's award-winning rums or enjoy an ice-cold Red Stripe beer as you gaze out at a flaming Caribbean sunset.

097

TREK ACROSS WADI RUM

JORDAN The compact Hashemite kingdom of Jordan is one of the best places to go trekking in the Middle East. Among the scattered monoliths of Wadi Rum, in the far south, the stark beauty of the country soaks into your soul. Getting out into the vast, echoing landscape of the desert has never been so easy: from Rum's Visitor Centre, a network of routes crisscrosses the desert floor and runs up, over or around eroded plateaus and rust-red cliffs. A bevy of local guides can lead you on foot to the towering hulk of Jebel Rum, and Ain Shalaaleh, a lush, shady spring known to Lawrence of Arabia; or out through the canyons of Jebel Umm Ashreen to scale the wind-sculpted dunes of Wadi Umm Ashreen.

098

SHOP AT A FAMOUS TRIBAL MARKET

LAOS As the sun sinks down into the mountains, casting a heavy glow over Laos' ancient capital, hundreds of crimson sheets are unfurled onto the pavements. Villagers from across the region quickly unpack their wares, setting the main street ablaze with colour, and Louang Phabang's famous tribal market is open for business. Find the quietest corner of the market, lit by a single electric bulb, where you'll come across some of Laos' most popular souvenirs: extraordinary dolls, painstakingly pieced together in a colourful tribute to the country's ethnic diversity. Each of the dazzling costumes signifies a different tribal group, and local materials are used to ensure complete authenticity. The bejewelled headdresses and dark pantaloons that represent the Akha hill tribe are among the bestselling pieces.

099

CHECK OUT THE CHAI IN INDIA'S DEEP SOUTH

INDIA The country's national drink is tea, or chai, grown on the border of Kerala and Tamil Nadu. Rising to well over 2500m, the wooded mountains here offer optimal conditions for tea cultivation, as the British were quick to discover. Vast swathes of virgin teak forest were clear-felled in the late nineteenth century to make way for plantations, and the hillsides here still support a giant patchwork of neatly cropped tea estates, interspersed with fragrant coffee and cardamom groves. Tea-picking is carried out by hand, usually by groups of women, whose dexterous fingers pick only the bud and first two leaves of each shoot before dropping them in a basket slung behind their backs.

100

EXPLORE THE ANCIENT TEMPLES OF ANGKOR

CAMBODIA Scattered over some four hundred square kilometres of countryside, the temples of Angkor are one of the world's great architectural showpieces – a profusion of ancient monuments remarkable both for their size and number, not to mention their incredible levels of artistry. An idealized representation of the Hindu cosmos in stone, they range from great pyramidal temple-mountains of Angkor Wat and Pre Rup through to the labyrinthine monasteries of Ta Prohm and Banteay Kdei. Magnificent to begin with, the ravages of time have added immeasurably to their appeal, with some individual monuments now swallowed by encroaching jungle – a far cry from the days of the Angkorian empire, when each temple was the centrepiece of a string of once bustling (but now vanished) villages, towns and miniature cities.

101

RIDE AROUND THE DESERT IN A DUNE-BUGGY

PERU In the northern reaches of the Atacama – the most arid desert on Earth – the lagoon at Huacachina appears like a mirage. An oasis of palm trees and blow-the-budget hotels, it lies hidden among massive sand dunes, some up to 300m high. During the late 1940s, the lagoon became one of Peru's most elegant resorts, and the area continues to draw the crowds, from cure-seekers to sand-surfers – you can rent wooden boards or foot-skis from the cafés along the shoreline. Hit the sand on a dune-buggy, an exhilarating experience that turns the vast, undulating mounds of sand into a giant roller coaster. And of course, pause to take in the stupendous view from the top of the dunes.

102

SKI FROM THE SKY IN BRITISH COLUMBIA

CANADA Heliskiing is a terrifically expensive, fairly dangerous but undeniably thrilling activity. From the air, you'll eagerly envisage making your signature squiggles and carve lines in the untouched powder fields. And as the helicopter recedes into the distance, leaving you alone atop the snowy peak, you'll feel every bit the pioneer. After you've adjusted to the rhythm and bounce of skiing this light powder, you're likely to discover that the deeper the snow and steeper the grade, the more exhilarating the run. Cornices and drop-offs that seemed forebidding from the helicopter will be a daring enticement; trees that from a distance looked impossibly dense reveal tempting paths; you'll drop into inclines that would have been unthinkable on harder snow, plunging in and out of chest-deep powder again and again.

103

EXPERIENCE THE MAJESTY OF THE BLUE MOSQUE

TURKEY With its six slender minarets and cascade of domes, the Blue Mosque is one of Istanbul's most striking monuments. Before construction began in 1609, objections were raised to the plan of a six-minareted mosque: it was said to be unholy to rival the six minarets of the mosque at Mecca. The true cause of the objections, however, probably had more to do with the need to bulldoze several palaces belonging to imperial ministers to make way for construction. Inside, take a moment to admire the predominantly blue colour of the ceiling, covered in some twenty thousand mosaic tiles – such a glorious sight that gazing up at them is well worth the neck-ache.

104

PARTY AT THE ATI-ATIHAN FESTIVAL

PHILIPPINES You need serious stamina for the three days and nights of nonstop dancing that mark the culmination of Ati-Atihan, the most flamboyant fiesta in the fiesta-mad Philippines. No wonder the mantra chanted by participants in this marathon rave is *hala bira, puera pasma*, which means "keep on going, no tiring". If you plan on lasting the course, start training now. Ati-Atihan, which takes place during the first two weeks of January in Kalibo – an otherwise unimpressive port town on the central Philippine island of Panay – actually lasts for two weeks. But it's the final three days that are the most important, with costumed locals taking to the streets in a riot of partying, music and street dancing.

SUNSET

Everything looks better at sunset, but everyone has a special one to remember: it could be eagles taking off from Atlantic cliffs, lions prowling at dusk in the Serengeti, or the tropical sky bursting into colour in the Maldives.

105
GO BIRDWATCHING AT CABO DE SÃO VICENTE

PORTUGAL The dramatic, cliff-fringed Cabo de São Vicente is the most southwesterly point of mainland Europe. The Romans called this Promontorium Sacrum and thought the sun plunged nightly into the sea here – it later became a Christian shrine when the relics of the martyred St Vincent were brought here in the eighth century. Today, tourist stalls selling trinkets line the approach road to a lighthouse – the most powerful in Europe – and a ruined sixteenth-century Capuchin convent, which survived the 1755 earthquake but not the dissolution of the monasteries in 1834. The sea off this wild set of cliffs shelters the highest concentration of marine life in Portugal, including rare birds such as Bonelli's eagle. Visit the cape at sunset when the views out across the water are breathtaking.

106
WATCH A TULIP BLOOM IN BUENOS AIRES

ARGENTINA Among the structures of Recoleta, Buenos Aires' grandest *barrio*, is the startling Floralis Genérica, a 25m aluminium and stainless-steel flower that opens and shuts. Donated in April 2002 by Argentine architect Eduardo Catalano, the Floralis Genérica is a tribute to all the world's flowers and, in Catalano's words, a symbol of "hope for the country's new spring" – a reference to the 2001 crisis, which saw widespread rioting in the capital. Watch the structure at sunset when a system of light sensors and hydraulics closes the six petals, before opening them again at 8am – the sculptor was afraid people would miss it if it opened at daybreak. The petals stay open all night on May 25, September 21 (the beginning of spring), Christmas Eve and New Year's Eve.

107

ADMIRE THE CHINESE FISHING NETS IN FORT COCHIN

INDIA The huge, elegant, and much-photographed Chinese fishing nets lining the northern shore of Fort Cochin are probably the single most familiar image of Kerala. Their history dates back to when the traders from the court of Kublai Khan are said to have introduced them to the Malabar region. Known in Malayalam as *cheena vala*, they can also be seen throughout the backwaters further south. The nets, which are suspended from poles operated by levers and weights, require at least four men to control them. The nets are best seen at sunset when the sky melds into a dusky pink hue, the glowing, reddy orb of the sun hovers behind the mesh of the nets, and the fishermen dart about in the foreground, preparing their boats to head out for a long night on the water.

108
ENJOY THE SUNSET AT KATA TJUTA

AUSTRALIA The "Many Heads", as Kata Tjuta translates from the local Aboriginal languages, are situated in the Uluru-Kata Tjuta National Park. Although many visitors will head straight to Uluru, don't miss this remarkable formation, which may once have been a monolith ten times the size of Uluru. The rock has since been carved by eons of weathering into 36 "monstrous domes", to use explorer Ernest Giles' words, each smooth, rounded mass divided by slender chasms or broader valleys. The composition of Kata Tjuta can be clearly seen in the massive, sometimes sheared, boulders set in a conglomerate of sandstone cement. Take in the awe-inspiring sight at the official viewing area as the sun goes down and watch as the rocks turn from deepest red to stunning silhouette.

109

GO FISHING ON ALASKA'S NAKNEK RIVER

USA The small bush community of King Salmon, Alaska, scattered alongside the broad Naknek River, was once a Cold War military base. Such is the remoteness, there's no reason to come here – except, perhaps, for some solitary sunset fishing. Some 22km downstream, the Bristol Bay fishing village of Naknek is the scene of the world's largest sockeye run, with over twenty million fish passing between mid-June and the end of July. Around seventy percent of the world's red salmon is caught in Bristol Bay, and three-quarters of those are fished out of the river in and around Naknek. Once the season starts, fishing boats are gunwhale to gunwhale, vying to be the first to get their nets in the water.

110

TAKE AN EVENING HIKE IN JOSHUA TREE NATIONAL PARK

USA The outdoors is one of California's treasures, and the state's fabulous parks come thick with superlatives: Sequioa National Park holds the largest trees in the world, Death Valley contains the lowest point in the Western Hemisphere, and both are rivalled by the extraordinary domes and spires of Yosemite. Serious desert enthusiasts should make a beeline for Joshua Tree National Park, a sublime place of crimson sunsets and weird cactus formations. Most cacti present few problems, but you should keep an eye out for the 2.5m cholla (pronounced "choy-uh"), or jumping chollas as some are called, because of the way segments seem to jump off and attach themselves to you if you brush past.

111

LOOK DOWN ON RIO DE JANEIRO

BRAZIL Sitting pretty on the western shores of near-landlocked Guanabara Bay, no other city in the world can compete with Rio de Janeiro's sensational combination of raw urban sprawl, sweeping sandy shoreline and lush jungle-clad mountains. The city's streets and buildings have been moulded around the mountain range, while out in the bay, rocky islands are fringed with fine white sand. Even the concrete skyscrapers that dominate the city's skyline manage to look magnificent against their verdant backdrop. At sunset it's easy to see why Rio's ten-million-strong citizens call it the Cidade Marvil: as dusk falls, look down on Rio, its city lights slowly gathering against the silky waters of the ocean and the surrounding dark shadowy hills.

112

SPOT WILDLIFE IN SERENGETI NATIONAL PARK

TANZANIA The Serengeti is one of the most famous wildlife areas in the world, in part due to its role right at the heart of the largest and most impressive animal migration on Earth. The Serengeti takes its name from the flat grassland plains that cover the eastern section, but in the north, rolling hills and thorny acacia woodland dominate. The area contains at least 28 acacia species, each adapted to a particular ecological niche, and the change in species is often startlingly abrupt. The undulating nature of the landscape makes it easy to spot animals from a distance, and you can see elephants, buffalos, zebras, gazelles and warthogs all year round. One of the best times to spot wildlife is in the early evening – an experience made even more special when teamed with a striking sunset.

113

TUCK IN TO FISH AND CHIPS BY THE SEASIDE

ENGLAND Despite it's name, Norfolk's Wells-Next-the-Sea, some eighty miles west of Blakeney, is actually a good kilometre or two from open water. In Tudor times, before the harbour silted up, this was one of the great ports of eastern England, a major player in the trade with the Netherlands. Today, the port is a shadow of its former self, but Wells – with its charming village and handsome beach backed by pine-clad dunes – is now a popular coastal resort. The quay, inhabited by a couple of amusement arcades and fish-and-chip shops, is a great place to try the quintessential English meal of fish and chips. On a warm summer evening, as the sun starts to dip, pop into a local "chippie" and tuck into some succulently fresh and perfectly battered fish.

114

WATCH THE SUN GO DOWN FROM BROOKLYN BRIDGE

USA Until the early 1800s, Brooklyn was no more than a group of autonomous towns and villages, but Robert Fulton's steamship service across the East River changed all that, starting with the establishment of a leafy retreat at Brooklyn Heights. What really transformed things, though, was the opening of the Brooklyn Bridge – at the time the largest suspension bridge in the world – on May 24, 1883. The beauty of the bridge itself and the spectacular views of Manhattan that it offers make a walk across its wooden planks an essential part of any New York trip. Make the bridge crossing at sunset to watch the sinking sun and see the city's skyscrapers silhouetted against an early evening sky.

115

SEE TRADITIONAL FISHERIES IN LOFOTEN

NORWAY Deep in the Arctic Circle, the skeletal curve of the Lofoten Islands stretches out across the Norwegian Sea. Snow-covered mountains loom behind small, laidback fishing villages. One of the most fascinating sights on the islands is the iconic rows of fish drying on traditional wooden racks. Go to see these at sunset, when the lowering sun's orange light makes an unusual latticework silhouette. You'll need to make sure that you go at the right time of year, though, because between late May and mid-July the sun never goes down, and the so-called "Midnight Sun" keeps the land in bright daylight. In the winter months, during "Polar Night", the sun does not even rise, and the swirling multicoloured Northern Lights put on a mesmerizing display instead.

116

STROLL THE BATTLEMENTS OF AN INDIAN FORT

INDIA Straddling the main Delhi–Mumbai train line, Gwalior is northern Madhya Pradesh's largest city and boasts one of India's most magnificent hilltop forts. The sandstone citadel, with its mighty turreted battlements encompassing six palaces and three temples, peers down from the edge of a sheer-sided plateau above the city's haze of exhaust fumes and busy streets. Two routes wind up the hill. In the west, a driveable track just off Gwalior Road climbs the steep gorge of Urwahi valley to the Urwahi Gate, passing a line of rock-cut Jain statues along the way. The other, more accessible, Gwalior Gate is on the northeast corner of the cliff. Time your visit with the sunset to see the sandstone glow in the early-evening light – there's also a nightly sound-and-light show in the Man Mandir palace.

117
JOIN A SUNSET BOAT CRUISE IN ZANZIBAR

TANZANIA Cradled by the monsoon winds, East Africa has been trading with the outside world for at least five millennia, though it was the Persians who introduced the dhow, the lateen-rigged vessel that became the maritime emblem of East Africa. At up to 15m in length, long-prowed jahazi dhows were the largest and grandest of East Africa's sailing ships; few are built today, but one or two examples can still be seen afloat. For those who prefer to explore Zanzibar's blissful coastline from above the water, rather than donning diving gear and delving deep into these rich coral reefs, a cruise on a dhow is ideal. For a classic African sundowner, hop on a boat with drink in hand and cruise about on the gentle waves, stained blood-red by the setting sun.

118
WATCH THE WORLD'S BIGGEST FOUNTAIN IN ACTION

DUBAI Dubai is like nowhere else. Often claimed to be the world's fastest-growing city, it has metamorphosed from a small Gulf trading centre to become one of the world's most glamorous, spectacular and futuristic urban destinations. Winding through the heart of Downtown Dubai is the large Burj Khalifa Lake, a section of which doubles as the spectacular 275m-long Dubai Fountain, the world's biggest, capable of shooting jets of water up to 150m high, and illuminated with over 6000 lights and 25 colour projectors. Arrive at the fountain as the sun sets; it really comes to life after dark, spouting carefully choreographed watery flourishes which "dance" elegantly in time to a range of Arabic, Hindi and classical songs, viewable from anywhere around the lake for free.

119

DINE WITH A VIEW IN BALI

INDONESIA On Bali, an island known for its special sunsets, you can be spoilt for choice when deciding where to watch the sun go down. One particularly attractive place to spend it is at Jimbaran Beach, where a handful of excellent seafood restaurants line the beachfront. Every morning at dawn the town's fishermen return with hundreds of kilos for sale at an enjoyable covered fish market in Kedonganan, at the northern end of the beach. It's at its best around 6–7am, but stays open all day – the stallholders are used to sightseers. Even if you don't see it, you can taste the day's catch when it is served at the dozens of beach *warung* that specialize in barbecued seafood. Pull up a chair, order some fresh lobster or red snapper and watch as the sun peacefully slips beneath the waves.

120
LISTEN TO THE SEA ORGAN IN ZADAR

CROATIA Alfred Hitchcock raved about sunsets in Zadar, and chances are you will be bowled over too, especially now the setting of the sun is accompanied by the sound effects of the so-called Sea Organ. As the sun drops, people gravitate to the peninsula's southwestern shoulder where the broad stone stairway descending to the sea was installed by local architect Nikola Bašić. The musical accompaniment has an unusual source: wave action pushes air through a series of underwater pipes and up through niches cut into the steps, producing a selection of mellow musical notes. The organ is at its best when the sea is choppy, but even during calm periods the tranquil notes of the organ will be sufficient to lure you into a meditative state.

121
FEEL INSIGNIFICANT AT THE GRAND CANYON

USA If a guidebook tells you that something is "impossible to describe", it usually means the writer can't be bothered to describe it – with one exception. After pondering the views of the Grand Canyon for the first time, the most spectacular natural wonder on Earth, most visitors are stunned into silence. The problem isn't lack of words. It's just that the canyon is so vast and so deep that the vista stretches so far across your line of vision, up, down and across, giving the impression of hundreds of kilometres of space. Distance becomes meaningless, depth blurs, and your sense of time and space withers away. On the canyon floor flows the Colorado River, its waters have carved out the gorge over five to six million years and exposed rocks that are up to two billion years old through vividly coloured strata. It's this incredible chromatic element that stays with you almost as much as the canyon's size, with the various layers of reds, ochres and yellows intensified at dusk as the sun illuminates the broken cliffs and towers. The Grand Canyon is like a mountain range upside down; the country around the top is basically flat and all the rugged, craggy elements are below you. The abruptness of the drop is bizarre and, for some, unnerving. But the Grand Canyon is like that: it picks you up and takes you out of your comfort zone, dropping you back just that little bit changed.

122

WITNESS THE GRANDEUR OF BAMBURGH CASTLE

ENGLAND One-time capital of Northumbria, the little village of Bamburgh lies in the lee of its magnificent castle. Solid and chunky, Bamburgh Castle is a spectacular sight, its elongated battlements crowning a formidable basalt crag high above the beach. Its origins lie in Anglo-Saxon times, but it suffered a centuries-long decline – rotted by sea spray and buffeted by winter storms, the castle was bought by Lord Armstrong (of Rothbury's Cragside) in 1894, who demolished most of the structure to replace it with a hybrid castle-mansion. Inside there's plenty to explore, including the sturdy keep with its unnerving armoury of pikes, halberds, helmets and muskets, the marvellous King's Hall and a medieval kitchen, complete with original jugs, pots and pans.

123

WATCH THE SUN SINK OVER SYDNEY HARBOUR

AUSTRALIA The Aussie city par excellence, Sydney stands head and shoulders above any other in Australia. Taken together with its surroundings, it's in many ways a microcosm of the country as a whole – if only in its ability to defy your expectations and prejudices as often as it confirms them. The Sydney Harbour Bridge, northeast of Circular Quay, has straddled the channel dividing North and South Sydney since 1932; eighty-plus years on, it is still the enduring symbol of the Sydney good life. The walk along the eastern side offers fabulous views of the harbour and the Opera House, particularly stunning when the sun goes down. Those with a head for heights can climb the bridge's 134m-high framework, scaling the steel arch to the summit – an excursion that's rewarded with 360-degree views of the city.

124

ESCAPE THE CROWDS AT THE PYRAMIDS OF GIZA

EGYPT Of the Seven Wonders of the ancient world, only the three great Pyramids of Giza have withstood the ravages of time. For millions of people, the Pyramids epitomize Ancient Egypt: no other monuments are so instantly recognized around the world. Yet comparatively few foreigners realize that there are at least 115 further pyramids spread across 70km of desert, from the outskirts of Cairo to the edge of the Fayoum Oasis. The mass of theories, claims and counterclaims about how and why the pyramids were built adds to the sense of mystery that surrounds them. During daytime, the tourist hordes dispel the mystique, but visit at sunset, dawn and late at night and you'll find that their brooding majesty returns.

125

TAKE A WALK ALONG THE BRIDGE OF ANGELS

ITALY The great circular hulk of the Castel Sant'Angelo, designed and built by Hadrian as his own mausoleum, marks the edge of the Vatican. Renamed in the sixth century, when Pope Gregory the Great witnessed a vision of St Michael here that ended a terrible plague, the papal authorities converted the building for use as a fortress and built a passageway to link it with the Vatican as a refuge in times of siege or invasion. The grand Ponte Sant'Angelo, lined by ten stunning angel sculptures, is a fitting walkway to the lavishly decorated rooms within the Castel Sant'Angelo. Once there, make sure you climb to the top for one of the best panoramas of Rome – a visit best timed with early evening for the wonderful views.

126

LOOK OUT TO SEA FROM ABERYSTWYTH PIER

WALES The liveliest seaside resort in Wales, Aberystwyth is an essential stop on the UK tourist trail. With two long, gentle bays curving around between twin rocky heads, Aberystwyth's position is hard to beat. The town, which is the capital of sparsely populated Mid-Wales, has a nice array of Victorian and Edwardian seaside trappings, including the Royal Pier, which has been a seafront landmark since it was erected as Wales' first purpose-built pleasure pier in 1865. It's a wonderful place to watch the sun dip over the horizon, turning the sky a pinky hue. As dusk gathers, shadows are cast over the dazzling, John Nash-designed Old College fronting the shingle beach. The Grade II listed pier's heyday may have long since passed, but plans are currently afoot for a renovation.

127

JOIN THE LOCALS AT CHOWPATTY BEACH

INDIA First impressions of Mumbai tend to be dominated by its chronic shortage of space, from its boulevards packed with streams of commuters, to its teeming bazaars. No surprise then that unwinding on Chowpatty Beach is a Mumbai institution. The beach comes to life in the evenings as the sun sets against an iconic background of the city's skyscrapers. People don't come to this long sandy stretch of beach to swim – the sea is notoriously polluted – but to wander, sit on the sand, have a massage, get their ears cleaned and gaze across the bay while the kids ride a pony or a rusty Ferris wheel. For an early-evening snack head to the end of the beach, where a row of *bhel puri* stalls hawk Mumbai's favourite sunset dish: crisp puffed rice with tamarind sauce, wrapped in a flat, fried *puri*.

128
SEE THE LOUVRE LIGHT UP

FRANCE The palace of the Louvre cuts a magnificent Classical swathe right through the centre of Paris – a fitting setting for one of the world's grandest art galleries. Originally little more than a feudal fortress, the castle was rebuilt in the new Renaissance style from 1546, under François I. Over the next century and a half, France's rulers steadily aggrandized their palace without significantly altering its style, and the result is an amazingly harmonious building. It wasn't until the building of I.M. Pei's controversial Pyramide in 1989 that the museum saw any significant architectural departure. The best time to view the outside is towards dusk on a sunny day, when the Pyramide sparkles in the setting sun and the Louvre is bathed in warm light.

129
ADMIRE THE Ō-TORII FLOATING GATE

JAPAN The one island of the Inland Sea you won't want to miss is Miyajima, just west of Hiroshima. The most famous attraction on Miyajima, officially known as Itsukushima, is the venerable ancient shrine of Itsukushima-jinja, where the vermilion Ō-torii gate, rising grandly out of the shallows (and seemingly floating on the sea), is considered to be one of Japan's most beautiful sights. Take in the view when the tide is high and the many day-trippers have left, and in the right light, you will be inclined to agree. Autumn is a particularly beautiful time to visit, when the myriad maple trees turn a glorious red and gold, perfectly complementing Itsukushima-jinja. Although the island is often swamped by visitors, it's a delightful place to spend the night.

130
WATCH A STONE AGE SUNSET IN ORKNEY

SCOTLAND Orkney is a unique and fiercely independent archipelago of seventy or so low-lying islands boasting a bevy of Stone Age settlements, such as Skara Brae's standing stones and chambered cairns. Orkney's most important Neolithic ceremonial complex is centred around the twin lochs of Stenness and Harray. On the thin strip of land between the two lochs stands the Ring of Brogdar, a wide stone circle dramatically sited on raised ground, which was originally surrounded by a henge, of which only the ditch survives today. The circle dates from before 2000 BC, and although only 27 of the 60 stones which once stood on the site remain, standing in the circle you'll feel a supremely atmospheric sense of space. Come here in time for sunset when the effect is truly stunning.

AFTER DARK

As night falls you'll find city skylines sparkling from Hong Kong to Chicago, street food tantalizing your tastebuds from Marrakesh to Laos, and partygoers filling the streets of Rio or lining up for the ultimate club night in Ibiza.

131

JOIN AN ALL-NIGHT PARADE IN RIO

BRAZIL If you thought Rio's Carnaval was just a three-day affair, think again. In no other country is the unbridled pursuit of pleasure such a national obsession, and Carnaval's status as the most important celebration on the Brazilian calendar entails a year's feverish preparation. Rio's samba schools recruit supporters in their thousands to help create the impossibly glitzy costumes, while flamboyant dances are choreographed by the school's director. During Carnaval itself, the city shuts up shop and throws itself into the most dazzling spectacle you're ever likely to see. In the evenings, hedonistic Carnaval balls extend well into the early hours, while some 50,000 people take part in the no-holds-barred, all-night *desfiles* (parades): a spectacular piece of street theatre unmatched anywhere else on Earth.

132

MARVEL AT THE GOLDEN ROCK AT DUSK

MYANMAR One of the holiest places in the country, Kyaiktiyo is a major draw for Buddhist pilgrims, with thousands visiting every day during the pilgrimage season. The site also pulls substantial numbers of non-believers, attracted by the pagoda's spectacular location, rising out of a huge gold-covered boulder – the Golden Rock – which is itself perched rakishly on a granite slab high up in the Eastern Yoma Mountains. It's rumoured to be possible to pass a thread between the rock and its base by rocking the boulder gently back and forth, and yet the Golden Rock has managed to withstand several large earthquakes in its long history. Pilgrims throng Kyaiktiyo both day and night, but activity is greatest early in the morning and at dusk, with people praying, lighting candles and making offerings.

133

MAKE A WISH AT THAILAND'S FESTIVAL OF LIGHT

THAILAND Every year on the evening of the full moon of the twelfth lunar month, Thais all over the country celebrate the end of the rainy season with Loy Krathong (the Festival of Light). One of Thailand's most beautiful festivals, it's held to honour and appease the spirits of the water. People set *krathongs* – miniature basket-boats made of banana leaves that have been elegantly folded and filled with flowers, sticks of incense and a lighted candle – afloat (*loy*) on the nearest body of water, to cast adrift any bad luck that may have accrued over the past year. It's traditional to make a wish as you launch your *krathong* and to watch until it disappears from view; if your candle burns strong, your wishes will be granted and you will live long.

134
ESCAPE THE CROWDS AT THE COLOSSEUM

ITALY The Colosseum is perhaps Rome's most awe-inspiring monument, an enormous structure that, despite nearly two thousand years of earthquakes, fires, riots and wars, still stands proud – a symbol not just of Rome, but of the entire ancient world. It's not much more than a shell now, eaten away by pollution and cracked by the vibrations of cars and the metro, but the basic structure is easy to see, and has served as a model for stadiums around the world ever since. You'll not be alone in appreciating it, and during summer the combination of people and scaffolding can make a visit more like touring a contemporary building site than an ancient monument. But visit late in the evening when it is quieter and the arena can seem much more like the marvel it really is.

135

JOIN THE HEDONISTS IN IBIZA

SPAIN Forget sleep and experience everything else to excess in Ibiza, the ultimate party island. Ibiza's clubbing scene is ludicrously out of proportion to its modest population, and in high season the superclubs have bloated capacities that need filling every day of the week. One of the strategies used by club promoters to publicize their nights are club parades: processions of costumed dancers bearing banners that weave through the labyrinthine lanes of the port area in Ibiza Town. Parades finish in Carrer d'Alfons XII, under the shadow of Ibiza's mighty medieval walls. Make sure you're there by 1am, when this small plaza is rammed with all manner of extrovert humanity, with an excess of drag queens, exposed flesh, and exhibitionists and fetishists of every sexual and satirical persuasion.

136

SEE THE EIFFEL TOWER AT ITS BEST

FRANCE Standing sentinel over a great bend in the Seine, the monumental flagpole that is the Eiffel Tower remains an endlessly inspirational sight, however tired of mega-monuments you may be. It's hard to believe that the quintessential symbol both of Paris and the brilliance of industrial engineering was designed to be a temporary structure for a fair. Late nineteenth-century Europe had a taste for giant-scale, colonialist–capitalist extravaganzas, but Paris's 1889 Exposition Universelle was particularly ambitious: when completed, the tower, at 300m, was the tallest building in the world. Walk past the Eiffel Tower after sunset, when, for the first ten minutes of every hour, thousands of effervescent lights scramble and fizz about the structure, defining the famous silhouette in luminescent champagne.

137
GO TO THE OPERA IN BEIJING

CHINA Plan a night at the Beijing Opera and marvel at the spectacle of one of China's most celebrated art forms. Decked out in an elaborate costume and a thick layer of make-up, Chinese opera performers use gesture, song, dance and martial arts in a highly stylized performance, whose every aspect is codified by convention and full of symbolism. Walking in a circle represents a long journey; to flick the sleeves means anger; upturned palms denotes embarrassment; and a character about to speak adjusts his headdress. The actor's aim is to instil beauty in every gesture, and, as in the forms of t'ai chi, to make smooth, sweeping movements and avoid the angular and abrupt. And all, of course, must be done in time to the din of percussive music.

138

TANTALIZE YOUR TASTE BUDS IN MARRAKESH

MOROCCO By day, much of Marrakesh's central square is resolutely Moroccan territory: tooth-pullers displaying neat piles of molars sit among scribes, street barbers, herb doctors and storytellers. Yet it's not till dusk that Jemaa El Fna really comes to life, its expanse filling with locals, tourists, musicians, acrobats and snake charmers. As the sun drops, the square becomes a huge open-air, lantern-lit dining area, packed with stalls which send plumes of cooking smoke spiralling up into the night. Head to one of the roof terraces overlooking the square to take in the magical scene below of gas lanterns twinkling through the haze. Then wander through the makeshift lanes of stalls to sample the endless variety of food on offer, everything from couscous and spicy merguez sausages to stewed snails and sheep's heads.

139

ADMIRE THE GOTHIC GRANDEUR OF BIG BEN AT NIGHT

ENGLAND At the south end of Whitehall is one of London's best-known monuments, the Palace of Westminster, better known as the Houses of Parliament. This is London's finest Victorian Gothic Revival building and symbol of a nation once confident of its place at the centre of the world. The original medieval palace burned down in 1834, and everything you see now – save for Westminster Hall – is the work of Charles Barry, who created an orgy of honey-coloured pinnacles, turrets and tracery. It's distinguished above all by the ornate, gilded clocktower popularly known as Big Ben, after the 13-tonne main bell that strikes the hour. It's a scene that's most impressive at night, when the building glows golden, its lights reflected in the dark waters of the Thames.

140

WITNESS MONTRÉAL'S MONTH OF FIREWORKS

CANADA Summer is a celebratory time in Montréal. After the winter hibernation, the locals spill onto the street terraces and fill the parks at the first sign of fine weather. Keen to milk it for all it's worth, the city lays on a series of spectacular firework displays, staged throughout July, which pay tribute to balmy nights in a normally frigid city. Montréal's International Fireworks Competition has become synonymous with summer in the city and sees music and dazzling pyrotechnics synchronized to tell a story, creating an ephemeral, somewhat surreal fantasy world. Fireworks companies representing different countries let off their arsenals at La Ronde – an amusement park on an island in the middle of the St Lawrence River – and the shows are stunningly artistic.

141

SOAK UP THE LAIDBACK VIBE IN CASTARA

TRINIDAD AND TOBAGO A picturesque fishing village, Castara's terrific beaches and chilled atmosphere have made it increasingly popular with visitors, but its remote location has so far saved it from being overrun by resorts. Fishing remains the main earner, and on the beach you can participate in the pulling of a seine net, still in constant use by the posse of Rasta fishermen. It's no surprise, then, that there's plenty of fresh fish to enjoy. Evenings are best spent savouring the excellent local cooking and soaking up the relaxed vibe around a beach bonfire. Come in August and things are more upbeat as revellers attending the Castara Fishermen's Fete – one of Tobago's biggest – flock to the beach; the drinking, dancing, eating and swimming start at midday and continue until well after dark.

142

TAKE A 360-DEGREE LOOK AT CHICAGO

USA In an architectural prize fight between America's biggest cities, there's little question that Chicago would win by a knockout, thanks to the sheer volume and variety of its grand buildings. At 344m, the Hancock Center offers a jaw-dropping 360-degree panorama – a good vantage point from which to take in lofty landmarks such as the ancient-looking Water Tower and the sleekly futuristic IBM Building. Climb 94 floors to the Hancock Center's observatory, which has an open-air viewing deck where winds can force the building to sway as much as 25cm from side to side, though the views of the city at night are so staggering you probably won't even notice. Walk two floors further up and you can take in the same panorama in comfort for the price of a drink.

143

CATCH TOKYO'S GIANT TUNA AUCTION

JAPAN Take advantage of your jetlag and join the queues – from 3am – for Tokyo's famous tuna auction. By 5am, the market is frenzied, with trucks and trolleys zipping around laden with man-sized fish, and feverish bidders clamouring for the best buys. Eels from Taiwan, salmon from Santiago and tuna from Tasmania are among the 480 different types of seafood – two thousand tonnes of it – that come under the hammer here daily. The headline tuna auctions, selling vast frozen fish that look like steel torpedoes, happen between 5.25am and 6.15am, and viewing, when allowed, is from within a cordoned-off area accommodating sixty people. As the commotion dies down, head for one of the area's plentiful sushi stalls servicing the sixty thousand people who pass through here each day.

144

BLAZE INTO THE NIGHT IN VALENCIA

SPAIN Join the people of Valencia to celebrate their patron saint's day and the passing of winter with a fiery party of ferocious proportions: ground-shaking fire-cracker fights, rockets booming overhead, billowing clouds of sulphurous smoke, and colossal bonfires on street corners that could cook your eyeballs from twenty metres. The main feature of Valencia's famous Las Fallas ("the fires") festival is the effigies, which come in all shapes and sizes, the most spectacular of them being enormous affairs. Almost four hundred are erected around the city, and as many as four hundred more in the surrounding towns and districts. Combine all this with the Spanish love of sangria, bravado and all-hours partying, and you get one hell of an early spring line-up that draws two million people from all over the world.

145

GET A TASTE FOR THE HIGH LIFE IN BANGKOK

THAILAND Bangkok boasts an astonishing fifty thousand places to eat, ranging from street-side noodle shops to the most elegant of restaurants. If you've had your fill of Thai street food, treat yourself to a taste of the high life: even if you don't splurge on one of the Lebua Hotel's extravagant suites, you can still mingle with the smart set at its rooftop Sky Bar, a standing-room-only roost above the city. Come around 6pm to take in the stunning, near-360-degree panoramas as day blends into night, with a pricey cocktail in hand. Also up here is Mediterranean Sirocco, which has the distinction of being the world's highest alfresco restaurant – at 275m above the pavements of Bangkok – but with views this spectacular, you'll hardly notice what's on your plate.

146
TRY STREET FOOD IN VIENTIANE

LAOS Set on a broad curve of the Mekong, Vientiane is perhaps Southeast Asia's most modest capital city. Though it may lack the buzz of Ho Chi Minh City or Bangkok, Laos's capital has been transformed in recent years from a desolate city of boarded-up shopfronts into a quaint backwater, with a string of cosmopolitan restaurants and cafés. It's a place for kicking back for a few days and taking life at a Lao pace – epitomized by sunset drinks on the banks of the Mekong and tasty, home-style cooking. Head to the riverside food stalls along the Mekong to try staples like *tam màk hung* (spicy papaya salad), *pîng kai* (grilled chicken) and crusty baguettes (*khào ji*) filled with Lao-style pâté, Vientiane's speciality snack.

147
SEE PETRA UNDER THE STARS

JORDAN Cut off by a barrier of rock and hidden in a valley at the heart of Jordan's Shara mountains, Petra's remote location has kept the ancient city cut off from the outside world and left somewhat shrouded in mystery. Time has worn at the soft sandstone of a city once powerful enough to challenge the might of Rome, but despite this the place remains legendary. Among its treasures Petra still boasts numerous classically carved facades, a massive theatre, huge Royal Tombs, the iconic Treasury, and the Monastery – Petra's largest monument – a building strikingly chiselled out of the mountainside. Seeing all the main sights can only just be squeezed into a long, tiring day – many people choose to stay longer and take the opportunity to explore further afield. Don't miss the chance to visit at night when the place dazzles under a starry sky and the light of thousands of candles – this is when the mystery of the place can be felt mostly keenly. Join the single-file procession as it makes its way through the Siq – the narrow, hidden gorge that stretches up to the entrance of the secretive city – which under the encroaching dusk is lit by twinkling candles. At the end of the path you'll arrive at the Treasury, the famous, jaw-dropping structure carved into the golden-hued cliff face. A Bedouin piper breaks the silence as crowds gather behind a blanket of flickering candles that cast an array of shadows, which flit across Petra's iconic facade.

148
ENJOY AN ALFRESCO DRINK IN RIO

BRAZIL Lapa is an old *bairro*; Brasil Gerson, writing in his *História das ruas do Rio de Janeiro*, noted that it was traditionally known as an "area of 'cabarets' and bawdy houses, the haunt of scoundrels, of gamblers, swashbucklers and inverteds and the 'trottoir' of poor, fallen women" – evidently a place to rush to, or avoid, depending upon your taste in entertainment. Until the mid-seventeenth century, Lapa was a beach, known as the "Spanish Sands", but development and land reclamation assisted its slide into shabby grandeur. More recently, things have been looking up, with the area blossoming into one of Rio's liveliest spots for an evening drink, especially at weekends, when its bars spill out onto the bustling streets.

149
REMEMBER, REMEMBER THE FIFTH OF NOVEMBER

ENGLAND Blazing stakes, flaming crosses and fireworks; celebrating Bonfire Night in Lewes will certainly set a pyromaniac's heart alight. The evening is a double whammy, commemorating both the foiling of the 1605 Gunpowder Plot and also honouring the seventeen Protestant martyrs burnt at the stake in the town in 1555–57. This is a festival steeped in history where paraders don medieval garb, light effigies of Guy Fawkes and the pope, and march through the streets grasping burning staffs. And the town's setting perfectly matches the historic mood: Lewes' old centre features numerous traces of its long past, with its Georgian buildings and network of "twittens" (narrow lanes), many of which are lined with crooked houses.

150
DRINK LIKE A LOCAL IN ISTANBUL

TURKEY With a population estimated at anything up to 25 million, Istanbul is a metropolis going on megalopolis, a vibrant urban centre that can make other European cities seem dull in comparison. It may have been stripped of its capital status back in 1923, but Istanbul still exerts a powerful, almost mystical, hold on the psyche of the nation. There's a buzz and confidence in the air that makes everything and anything seem possible – and nowhere is this more palpable than in the Balik Pazarı (Fish Market). Join hordes of Istanbullu at the weekend to gorge on heaps of meze and fish specialities and down copious amounts of rakı in rowdy *meyhanes* (taverns), before singing and dancing along to roving bands of Roma musicians.

151
GO TO A TANGO SHOW

ARGENTINA Visiting a dark and romantic tango hall and watching the nation's famous sultry dance is one of the best ways to spend an evening in Buenos Aires. From smart performances in grand old theatres with plush dining alongside, to more intimate sessions in cosy little venues, there's a whole host of shows on offer across the city. Tango shows may be expensive, but you'll get to see a series of top tango dancers in one evening, and many are well worth the splurge. After the show, if you are feeling inspired by what you've seen, then head to one of the city's *milongas* – regular dance clubs that are popular with tango dancers of all ages. Usually these start with lessons at the beginning, giving you time to find your feet.

152
KEEP UP WITH MADRID'S NIGHTLIFE

SPAIN Whatever Barcelona or San Sebastián might claim, the Madrid scene, immortalized in the movies of Pedro Almodóvar, is still the most vibrant in Spain. As you get to grips with the city, you soon realize that it's the lifestyle of its inhabitants – the *madrileños* – that makes the capital such a fun place to be. The nightlife is a pretty serious phenomenon: the *madrileños* are nicknamed *los gatos* or "the cats" for their nocturnal lifestyle, and the roads can be gridlocked in the early hours of the morning, when locals are either heading home or moving on to the dance-past-dawn clubs. You'll need to prepare yourself to keep up, as the *madrileños* play hard and very late in a thousand bars, clubs, discos and *tascas*.

153
EXPERIENCE HOI AN'S FULL-MOON FESTIVAL

VIETNAM Banish thoughts of glow-paint ravers and blasting music on crowded Thai beaches, Vietnam's Full-Moon Festival in Hoi An is a much more sophisticated affair. Every month on the fourteenth day of the lunar calendar, the charming little city switches off its street lights and the centre closes to traffic. As dusk encroaches, the city is transformed into a magical scene as hundreds of glowing silk lanterns light the narrow alleys, hang from the wooden-fronted shophouses and line the banks of the Thu Bon River. By nightfall, performers and food stalls have filled the cobbled streets and people have gathered along the riverbank to set tiny flickering candles adrift on the lazy waters.

154

ADMIRE SINGAPORE'S TOWERING SKYLINE

SINGAPORE A dazzling shrine to consumerism, Singapore's skyline is best admired at night. And no place is better to admire the views than Marina Bay, a feat of engineering which was created by building three massive expanses of reclaimed land and the sealing off of the Singapore and Kallang rivers from the sea. The Marina Bay Sands resort dominates the area, its rooftop restaurants and bars boasting jaw-dropping panoramic views of the city's skyline; at night a stunning display of glittering skyscrapers and lights is mirrored in the waters of the marina below. Also worth a visit are the nearby Gardens by the Bay, a futuristic – almost alien – world of colourfully lit tree-like structures that stretch up to the night sky.

155

PARTY WITH DUTCH COURAGE IN AMSTERDAM

THE NETHERLANDS Sex clubs, gay clubs, tourist hubs and superclubs – Amsterdam nightlife is many things to many people, a wonderfully eclectic mix that both meets and surpasses visitors' expectations of sex, drugs and hard-house. As in London or New York, Amsterdam's superclubs pull in the young, the beautiful and the cutting edge, but the key difference is the freewheeling Dutch attitude of inclusion. Don't miss the annual King's Day celebrations at the end of April, one of the hottest events on the club calendar, when the street party spills over into two nights of flamboyant debauchery that rivals anything Rio has to offer. Shake off your preconceptions, don an orange wig, and you'll soon be welcomed into the fray as an honorary Amsterdammer.

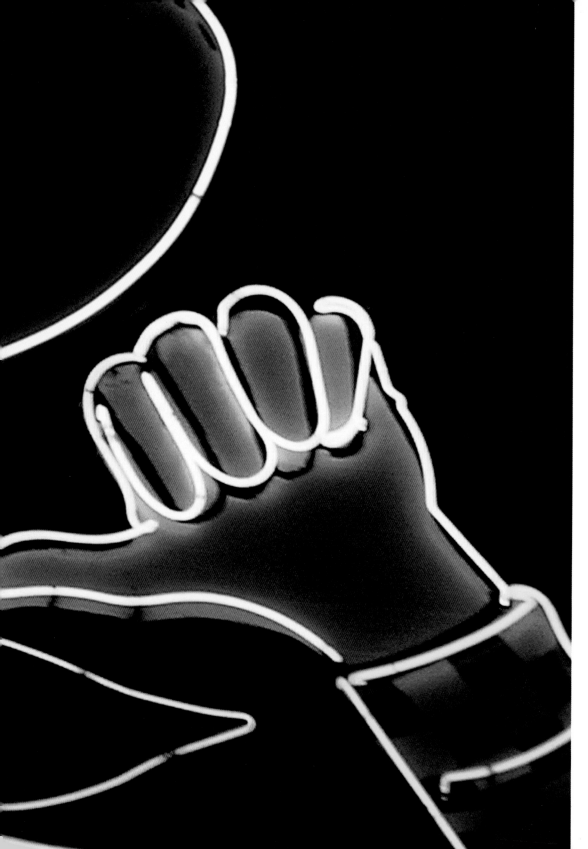

156
TRY YOUR LUCK IN LAS VEGAS

USA Las Vegas has always had a ruthless streak. The rough-and-ready frontier town squeezed itself into a tux when Frank Sinatra and his Rat Pack ruled the roost, slipped into a toga when the 1960s turned decadent, and even slapped on the greasepaint during its brief bid to reinvent itself as a great place to bring the kids. These days, everything is bigger and shinier than ever, and the new watchwords seem to be sophistication, elegance and opulence. Stray away from the Strip and you'll find what little old-style neon still survives, now appealing largely to nostalgics who feel the modern city has strayed too far from the no-nonsense populism of its early years. You can even pay your respects to long-abandoned neon masterpieces in a "Neon Boneyard".

157

ADMIRE THE NORTHERN LIGHTS IN SWEDISH LAPLAND

SWEDEN The Northern Lights may be elusive, but with 24 hours of darkness at the peak of winter in Swedish Lapland, at least time will be on your side. Embrace the long nights by heading out into the frozen darkness to try and catch this breathtaking spectacle. These soft, flickering wisps of colour are caused by solar particles hitting the earth's atmosphere: each hue – from pale green to dark pink – is produced by a different element. It's best to give yourself a week or two for a good chance of seeing them; pitch a tent, bring a sturdy tripod and keep your fingers crossed (inside a good pair of mittens) for cloudless skies.

INDEX

PICTURE CREDITS

The publisher would like to thank the following for their kind permission to reproduce their photographs:

p.10 & p.4 Dreamstime.com: Galyna Andrushko
p.42 Dreamstime.com: Clickit
p.43 Dreamstime.com: fstockfoto
p.55 PunchStock: Digital Vision
pp.62–63 Dreamstime.com: Zahorec
pp.64–65 Greg Dickinson
p.73 Olivia Rawes
p.78 Alamy Images: Martin Strmiska
p.87 Olivia Rawes
p.92 & p.4 Greg Dickinson
p.97 Olivia Rawes
p.102 Dreamstime.com: Patryk Kosmider
pp.118–119 Keith Drew
p.126 Dreamstime.com: Rudmer Zwerver
p.128 Greg Dickinson
pp.130–131 Dreamstime.com: Erdal Acanal

p.134 Olivia Rawes
p.140 Dreamstime.com: Tatonka
p.142 & p.4 Dreamstime.com: Kurira
pp.144–145 Dreamstime.com: Michal Knitl
pp.150–151 Keith Drew
pp.162–163 Dreamstime.com: Steve Rosset
pp.166–167 Dreamstime.com: Elena Frolova
pp.168–169 Dreamstime.com: Inga Ivanova
pp.172–173 Olivia Rawes
p.177 Dreamstime.com: Ryan Deberardinis
pp.178–179 Dreamstime.com: Ekaterinabelova
pp.194–195 & p.4 Fotolia: Galyna Andrushko
pp.198–199 Dreamstime.com: Anthony Ngo
p.206 Paris Tourist Office
pp.208–209 Dreamstime.com: John Braid
pp.214–215 Dreamstime.com:
 Edwardroom501

pp.222–223 Dorling Kindersley: Alan Keohane
p.224 Dreamstime.com: Marc Pinter
p.225 Dreamstime.com: Mircea Costina
pp.228–229 Dreamstime.com: Shelley Coleman
p.248 Dreamstime.com: Jacetan
pp.252–253 & p.4 Dreamstime: Jensottoson

Sunrise opening image Fisherman on Inle Lake, Myanmar © Dorling Kindersley: James Tye
Daytime opening image Joshua Tree National Park, USA © Rough Guides: Paul Whitfield
Sunset opening image Stilt houses, the Maldives © Dreamstime.com: Vling

After dark opening image Hong Kong skyline © Rough Guides: Tim Draper
Front cover Kayaking on Trillium Lake, USA © AWL Images: Danita Delmont Stock
Back cover Rio de Janeiro at sunset, Brazil © Dreamstime.com: Ekaterinabelova
Inside front flap (US edition) Petra at night, Jordan © Rough Guides: Jean-Christophe Godet
Inside back flap (US edition) Fisherman on Inle Lake, Myanmar © Dorling Kindersley: James Tye

All other images © Dorling Kindersley and © Rough Guides
For further information see: **dkimages.com**